A Feather for Daedalus

Explorations in Science and Myth

Kim Malville
University of Colorado

Cummings Publishing Company, Inc.
Menlo Park, California • Reading, Massachusetts
London • Amsterdam • Don Mills, Ontario • Sydney

To Kathy and Leslie

Cover Photo
"The Pleiades Cluster," by Lick Observatory

Acknowledgment is made to the following source for the illustration on p. 113.

From *Winnie-the-Pooh* by A.A. Milne, illustrated by Ernest H. Shepard. Copyright, 1926, by E.P. Dutton & Co. Renewal, 1955, by A.A. Milne. Reprinted by permission of the publishers, E.P. Dutton & Co., Inc.

Cummings Publishing Company, Inc.
2727 Sand Hill Road
Menlo Park, California 94025

Preface

The primary concern of *A Feather for Daedalus: Explorations in Science and Myth* is to reaffirm the central location of mankind in science. While man is central in his art and mythology, his role in science has been poorly articulated. We seem to have lost sight of the main actor for he has been upstaged by his own scientific creations. In this book, the spotlight is clearly focused upon man and his fertile mind.

Because of my own background, I have drawn extensively from physics and astronomy for examples of creative science with the result that the book is most appropriate as a supplement to introductory courses in astronomy and physics. However, because of the cooperative nature of our quest, the material should be appropriate for any science course in which the humanistic implications of science are sought. Courses in philosophy and religion might find it a useful bridge between science and the humanities. Although some rather sophisticated concepts in modern physics and astronomy are considered, the book can be understood comfortably by the general reader.

More specifically, Chapter One introduces Daedalus as the mythical guide for our journey away from the traditional and mechanistic aspects of science, and it introduces the possibilities of creative mythmaking in today's science. Chapter Two explores the richness of a universe which yields an infinite number of phenomena that appear both as physical fact and human metaphor. The mythological dimensions of modern science especially evidenced by our search for unity in the universe are treated in Chapter Three. Chapter Four is concerned with the intuition of guiding pathways in our surrounding space-time as expressed in both myth and science. Chapter Five describes the struggles for individualization of creators of science such as Copernicus and Kepler. Our freedom to renovate traditional ideas and construct new models in science is discussed in Chapter Six. Chapter Seven treats the importance of realizing that our science will eventually be found to be incomplete and erroneous as both we and our universe change with time. Chapter Eight concludes the book with a discussion of the human uses of complementarity and suggests a resolution of some of the paradoxes of modern science.

My debt is great to the many students who have helped me develop the ideas and the general approach of this book. A portion was written during one summer when I was supported by the High Altitude Observatory of the National Center for Atmospheric Research. I wish to thank its director, Gordon Newkirk, for his encouragement.

Contents

"The topic for today is: What is reality?"

Chapter One
Where the Labyrinth Ends

The Flight of Daedalus

According to legend, Daedalus escaped from the island kingdom of Crete with wings of feathers held together with wax. One suspects that his wings were nothing that simple or elegant, but instead had a power and magic far beyond the crude ingredients which were more likely mite-infested feather quills, chewing gum, sticky tape, and rubber bands. But the important point is that Daedalus escaped from his prison and from the horrors he had assisted in creating.

In many ways Daedalus was an archetypal scientist, innocently dedicated to the ethics of his craft and not his time, and willing to work for whomever would let him explore the fantasies of his mind and the wonders of the world. Daedalus is known for three major inventions: his wings, the labyrinth, and the upholstered wooden cow which started it all.

Daedalus had been delighting the family of King Minos with the animated wooden dolls he had been carving. It was during this time that Queen Pasiphaë fell passionately in love with a dazzling white bull which Poseidon had given to Minos as a sign for the people of Crete that Minos was the rightful king, with the understanding that he would sacrifice the animal soon after becoming king. Minos, however, was so struck by the handsome creature that he sacrificed another bull in its stead, hoping that the god would not be disturbed by such little deceit. Poseidon was disturbed, and in his wrath caused Pasiphaë to be attracted to the snow-white bull from the sea. At her request, Daedalus carved a life-sized wooden cow, upholstered with cowhide, with little doors in the back through which Pasiphaë could enter. It was a clever invention, as exciting a challenge for the craftsman Daedalus and as tragic a misuse of man's talents as have been the atom bomb and the chemicals used for defoliating the jungles of Asia.

One fine morning, the surrogate cow containing Pasiphaë was seductively rolled into the meadow where the bull was grazing. She caught his eye, had her passion satisfied, and in due course gave birth to the Minotaur, a half-man, half-bull monstrosity. The people of Crete were ashamed and afraid of this creature whose cries at night were indistinguishable from the roar of the earthquake, and Daedalus was called in by Minos to design a vast labyrinth with winding, blind passages in which the monster could be hidden. Daedalus was again trapped by his talents: the labyrinth was as unbecoming a human creation as the handcrafted cow. Every year Athenian youths were pushed into the labyrinth as a sacrifice to the Minotaur. The tragedy was great for Daedalus, as Athens was his home.

Before escaping from Crete he showed Ariadne, the daughter of Minos and the sister of the Minotaur, a secret door leading into the maze. He gave her a ball of string which, if one end was tied at the entrance, would roll by itself twisting and turning to the inner recesses of the labyrinth where the Minotaur lived. Later, when Theseus came to Crete to kill the Minotaur, Ariadne gave him the ball of string, the end of which he tied to the entrance of the labyrinth. He thus was able to find his way out after he had killed the Minotaur. Then, thanks to Daedalus' cleverness, Theseus and his friends escaped from the island, taking Ariadne with them.

Daedalus has walked many times on this earth since the days of Crete, and the world has seen many Minotaurs and labyrinths. There have also been a few flights with wings of ingenuous and varied constructions, many of which started with a craftsman innocently carving wooden dolls. What makes the original Daedalus a unique and valuable guide for our journey is not that he could carve skillfully and build labyrinths. Many have done that. Daedalus, however, was able to undo some of the mischief of his science and free both himself and the island of the curse from his misapplied talents.

Waves, Particles, and Machines

For us living in the twentieth century, entrapment in our labyrinths has occurred in varied and subtle ways. Because we have been trapped by an overly rigid and authoritative world view handed to us by our parents, clergy, and teachers, we have been prevented from discovering alternate modes of perception. The scientific community has done its share of labyrinth-building by encouraging belief in the essential truthfulness of modern physical science.

But it is our love for mechanical models that has been most responsible for imprisoning modern man. The overwhelming success of the mechanical and mathematical style of science introduced by Galileo and Newton left its imprint upon the consciousness of the world as our self-conception correspondingly shrank to the finiteness of the machine. Who would dare challenge the authority of the master model-builder of all time, Isaac Newton? His inventions, the mathematics of calculus, the laws of motion, and the law of universal gravity all describe a cosmic machine so flawless and so well conceived that it should never falter or err.

It was a frictionless perpetual motion machine that Newton fashioned as a model for our universe. Once started it should continue in a perfectly predictable fashion. It was a deterministic cosmos since the future was fully determined by the past. Chaos was replaced by a clean, well-lighted labyrinth with the monster of predestination at its center. This windup universe of Newton was extraordinarily successful, lasting, during its 250-year lifetime, far longer than most windup toys. However, toward the end of the nineteenth century as conflicting observations and experiments began to appear, it started to behave erratically. By the 1920s, due partly to the development of quantum mechanics and relativity, the world machine had stopped running entirely. But the old ways have been hard to discard, and today, despite all of the recommendations from physics to the contrary, we still carry an image of a gigantic machine as our model for the objective world.

As an example of how *unmachinelike* our present conception of reality is, consider the quantum mechanical picture of light. Dur-

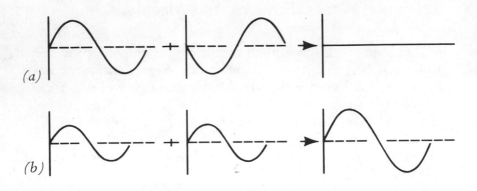

Figure 1-1. (a) Destructive interference. (b) Constructive interference.

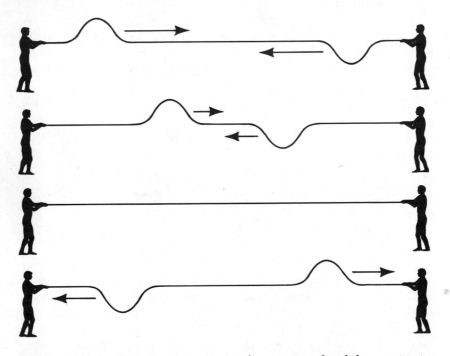

Figure 1-2. The disappearing wave trick: an example of destructive interference of wave pulses.

ing the last seventy years, physics has discovered that light must be viewed as both wave and particle. At first this concept seems strange; waves and particles are different, and we had expected less ambivalent answers from the physicists. A particle is like a baseball: it is localized in space, and there is no doubt when one is holding it in his hand. Conversely, a wave extends over space. When there are waves in a swimming pool, the entire pool is "waving." There is no way to "catch" the waves by collecting anything less than all the water in the pool. In a strange and stubborn way, light shares the characteristics of both waves and particles; it resists being placed in just one category. No machine lurks in the paradoxical behavior of light; no single blueprint exists for the wave-particle duality of light. The distinction between waves and particles needs to be clearly demonstrated, for these two complementary ways of describing the world are at the basis of the revolutionary mode of thinking known as quantum mechanics.

Waves in water or waves in a shaken rope transfer energy. When two people are holding a rope and one person shakes his end, the other person soon finds that his hand is shaking. Energy has been transferred along the rope. So too, water waves such as *tsunamis* can carry as much destructive energy as atomic missiles.

Waves interact with each other, either adding or subtracting energy. Here indeed is a trick particles cannot perform. If a wave crest flows into the trough of another wave of equal amplitude, they cancel each other by *destructive interference* (Figure 1-1a). If, on the other hand, two wave crests meet and join, they add to form a mound of water twice as high as the original individual waves (Figure 1-1b). Such is the benefit of *constructive interference;* such is the advantage of being a wave. In contrast, of course, two trains traveling toward each other on the same track will neither constructively nor destructively interfere, but merely demolish each other, never to travel again. Waves in a rope, however, can destructively interfere as they meet in the middle and then moments later reappear and continue down the rope (Figure 1-2).

Not only can two waves interfere with each other, but one wave can interfere with itself. If light from a lamp passes through a filter transmitting only one color so that the waves have only one specific wavelength and if that light then passes through a long

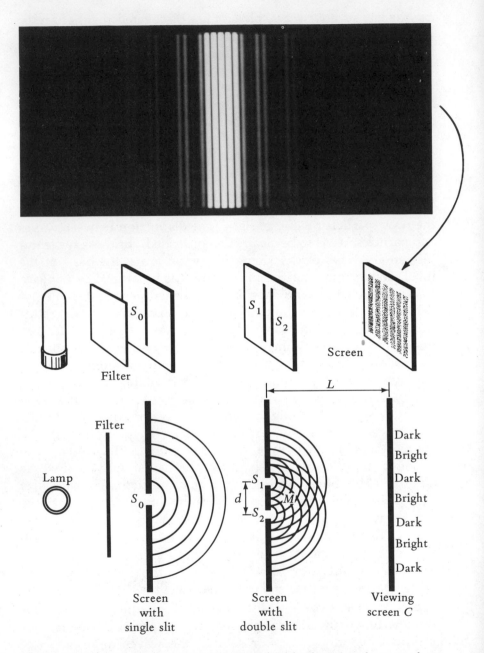

Figure 1-3. The interference pattern for a double slit. The photograph is an enlarged detail of the screen. (Photograph from Bruno Rossi, *Optics*, 1957, Addison-Wesley, Reading, Mass.)

narrow slit (slit S_0 in Figure 1-3), that light is now coherent — everywhere within one wave front either "going up" or "going down" together. If this coherent light then passes through two more narrow slits, S_1 and S_2, each of those slits acts as a second source, and the light coming from these two slits interferes both constructively and destructively with itself (Figure 1-3). As seen projected on a screen beyond the two slits, there are streaks of brightness and darkness which are parallel to the long dimension of the slits. They are bright where the waves of light have added to each other and dark where they have subtracted. In this instance light is clearly behaving as a wave. The same effect occurs when parallel ocean waves pass through two breaks in a sea wall.

When one of the slits is closed so that light can pass through only the other slit, these bright and dark streaks disappear and the screen is illuminated by diffuse light which is brightest directly beyond the slit (Figure 1-4a). Remarkably, the brightness of the screen at the position of one of the previously dark streaks actually increases when one of the slits is closed. This brightening would be extremely hard to understand if light consisted of particles. The closing of one of the slits should halve the number of particles reaching the screen (Figure 1-4b). Since the space between the slits and the screen would be less crowded with particles, the screen should be darker throughout. Because it is brighter at certain places, it is certain that light *cannot* be made up of particles.

Now, feeling quite confident that light is a wave, let us examine the *photoelectric effect*. When light falls upon a metal surface which contains electrons in large numbers, some of the electrons can be ejected from the surface due to the action of the light (Figure

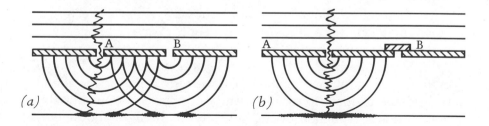

Figure 1-4. The effect of closing one slit in double slit interference. (a) Interference pattern due to two slits. (b) Elimination of the interference pattern when one slit is closed.

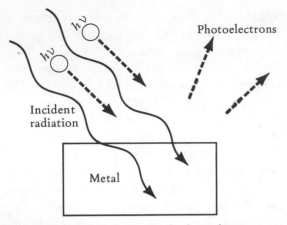

Figure 1-5. The ejection of photoelectrons from an illuminated metallic surface.

1-5). The energy of the ejected electrons should depend upon the energy of the incident beam of light. If ocean waves, for instance, are breaking on a concrete wall, the wall can be broken if the waves have sufficient height; if a wave crest contains enough energy to overcome the cohesive energy of the concrete, then the concrete may be torn apart by the waves. The energy of a wave is proportional to the speed of up-and-down motion. The speed of a piece of flotsam bobbing up and down on a water wave is a measure of the energy carried by the wave. Likewise, the speed of a chunk of ice in a glass of Coca-Cola is determined by how much energy we are putting into the act of shaking the glass. As we shake the glass more and more furiously the ice will soon fly out; the speed of that flying chunk of ice will be large if we have put a lot of energy into shaking the glass.

The same effect should occur in a light wave when an electron is jiggled up and down by the electric field of the wave. The energy of that up-and-down motion is proportional to the intensity of the light. Thus, a beam of high intensity light falling on a metal should induce large-amplitude jiggling of the electrons in the metal and cause some of them to escape with large speeds. We would also predict that a reduction of the intensity of the light should correspondingly reduce the energy of the liberated electrons.

When we actually perform the experiment, we discover results which completely conflict with our predictions. When the metal is illuminated with light of one color, or frequency ν, all of the ejected electrons acquire the same energy $E = h\nu$, regardless of the intensity of the light. Only the *color* of the light counts. When the light is very dim, the ejected electrons have the same energy, but there are fewer of them.

So our predictions have completely failed. The photoelectric effect indicates that light does not consist of waves. The results can be understood if light consists of swarms of particles of energy $E = h\nu$ such that when one of these particles hits an electron it is ejected with the energy $h\nu$. When the beam of light is weak, it contains few such particles or photons, and since each knocks out an electron of energy $E = h\nu$ there are fewer such electrons. The intensity of the beam determines the number but not the energy of the electrons. This behavior can be understood only if light consists of discrete pulses of energy, or photons.

Therein lies the strange and marvelous paradox of light. One type of experience demands that light be wavelike and not particles; another demands that it be composed of particles and not waves. It seems that the answers returned to us are determined by the nature of our questions. Particle-evocative questions produce particlelike behavior; likewise for wave-evocative questions. We ask, "Are you a wave?" to which is answered, "Yes, I am a wave." "But," we ask, "are you not also a particle?" and hear, "Yes, I am a particle." It seems that we know just two kinds of questions, and whenever we call, the appropriate phenomenon emerges from its den. Other creatures would perhaps emerge if we knew how to summon them, but we do not know the words.

Here indeed is a phenomenon far different from any machine we have ever encountered or would care to ride in. This schizophrenia of light is so different from what we had expected to find in mechanistic physics. The warning is clear: we cannot describe our reality as a big machine containing a multitude of smaller machines. Some other model is needed, and we wait for Daedalus the explorer and visionary.

Reconciliation and Scientific Metaphor

The flight of Daedalus was that of an adventurer willing to press beyond the campfire circle into the trackless forest. His were the wings of extraordinary science, rarely heard in the air but which have led to such flights as those of Newton, Einstein, Bohr,

Schrödinger, and others. They were flights away from the familiar and secure; they were excursions of creative mythology by individuals free to explore the infinite temples of their humanness.

The creative mythmaking of today's science is an adventure in reconciliation: the marriage through metaphor of the diverse and seemingly incompatible aspects of the world. Since the metaphor links different aspects of the world, scientific laws and theories are the epoxy, glue, and sticky tape of our lives. By attempting to demonstrate the relatedness of the facts of the world, science reconciles those items which previously may have appeared alien to each other. The world was given to mankind in the form of disconnected facts and unrelated images, often in apparent conflict: tigers appeared, snow fell, rivers overflowed their banks, comets appeared in the sky, and people were caught up in the cycles of birth and death. And the world remained like disorderly fragments until viewpoints were discovered which allowed the resolution of the parts.

Those philosophers who express outrage at the so-called reductionist approach of science — who fear a world reduced to its fundamental laws with no place in it for human values — miss the sense in which these laws are the keys to that magic act of reconciliation. Equally mistaken are those people who maintain that we must cease trying to discover new laws and work instead to prevent those laws we already possess from destroying us. Much of the beauty and coherence of our world has been generated by those individuals who struggled to find the key pieces in our cosmic puzzle. The fruit of their struggle — our laws of physics — are not authoritative injunctions handed down from the gods. For those who allow themselves to be open and receptive, these laws can achieve a magnificent harmonizing of the world. Through them the wholeness of the world becomes accessible and authentic. That they never become absolute is of no consequence; the world changes with time, and soon new laws will be necessary to affirm its wholeness.

The growth of our modern science continues as we refine our old metaphors and discover how to draw more and more of the facts of the physical universe into authentic relationships with each other. Our theories and laws link the facts we have at our disposal. We judge them to be authentic if they are consistent with the continuing flow of new facts which pour into our field of vision.

Yet few people understand the subjective and human quality of the great works of science. The masterpieces of modern science such as general relativity or quantum mechanics are no more truthful and no more alien than the masterpieces of literature and music which can sometimes affect us so deeply. We should be able to look at the theory of general relativity and say, "Ah, that is the creation of a man, a marvelously talented man. How did he manage to do it?" In the same way we should be awestruck that Beethoven could have written his symphonies. Both creations are demonstrations of mankind's extraordinary powers for creating new metaphors. Yet too often we separate Beethoven and Einstein and judge their creations to be of different character. We have not found a way of participating in science as we participate in music or art. This lack of participation in our scientific mythologies has been one of the sources of that collection of problems associated with the schizophrenic split of our culture into the scientific and nonscientific.

Yet participation remains an unrealized opportunity. A fully assembled machine does not invite participation. But the scientific world view is always in the process of unfolding and always has that sense of openness such as we encountered in the wave-particle duality of the photon. In our enthusiasm for the success of our science, we have neglected to emphasize its incompleteness. Because we have gathered data from such an infinitesimal fraction of the total universe, our most powerful theories are only a partial representation of the reality which resides in the vastness of space. We are, after all, newcomers to our universe, since we have been gathering our scientific facts for only a few hundred of the ten billion years of the universe's existence. By acting as guides rather than providing definitive answers, our scientific theories can lead to realities beyond themselves.

Science — this precocious child we do not exactly know how to live with — can be used for more than the construction of warheads, the design of rockets, or the invention of technological marvels. As we shall attempt to demonstrate, the insights of science can be used in the same manner that we use our religious and artistic symbols — as evocative devices to lead us beyond that which is merely said.

We have to a certain extent been guilty of misusing our science in the production of upholstered gadgets and computerized wonders, thus neglecting it as an aid for mankind's larger journey. It is as though after hacking our way through the forest we have reached the shore of a great river which prevents us from proceeding further. The water's edge contains many beautiful and fascinating pebbles. Their colors and shapes are extraordinary! Never before on our journey have we seen such marvelous pebbles. They are, in fact, so captivating that we have completely forgotten about our journey. Instead we spend all of our time gathering these brightly colored rocks — the *facts* with which we have become so infatuated of late. Into higher and higher piles we gather these facts, never wanting to stray too far from them for fear that someone might take them from us. And so we remain, trapped by our pebbles, unable to use them because we are too busy collecting others, and we are unable to explore the rest of the world. We could, it is true, use our rocks to continue on our journey by tossing them into the stream ahead of us and using them as stepping stones. Shall we?

Splash . . . . . .

. . . the mechanistic point of view involves the assumption that the possible variety in the basic properties and qualities existing in nature is limited so that one is permitted at most to consider quantitative infinities which come from making some finite number of kinds of things bigger and bigger or more and more numerous . . . (However) . . . as far as the empirical data of science themselves are concerned, they cannot justify any a priori restrictions at all . . . of the inexhaustibly rich and diversified qualities and properties that may exist in nature.

David Bohm

David Bohm, *Causality and Chance in Modern Physics*, Philadelphia: University of Pennsylvania Press, 1957.

Chapter Two

The Compleat Universe

One Toss of the Cosmic Dice

The river, deep within its canyon, flows to the sea. "Love this river, stay by it, learn from it," the river says to the Siddhartha of Herman Hesse.[1]*A certain path has been chosen by the water. The path is the result of a series of subtle forces working on the moving water: a slight irregularity in the valley floor sends the water in one direction; a sudden rush of wind on a wave crest encourages the water off in another; a pile of rocks or a collection of driftwood turns the water in still another direction. Gradually the water finds the sea. If the gradient of the land is steep and the flow of water is abundant, the stream digs deeply into the valley floor. The river has decided; its route is fixed. Opportunities for another curve or another series of rapids elsewhere in the floor of the valley have been passed over and shall never occur again.

Siddhartha, sitting on the bank of the river, catches a glimpse of the universe and the people contained by it: "They all become part of the river. It was the goal of all of them, yearning, desiring, suffering, and the river's voice was full of longing, full of smarting woe, full of insatiable desire. The river flowed on towards its goal. Siddhartha saw the river hasten, made up of himself and his relatives and all the people he had ever seen. All the waves and the water hastened, suffering, towards the goals, many goals, to the waterfall, to the sea, to the current, to the ocean and all goals were reached and each one was succeeded by another."[2]

Siddhartha sees but one universe in the river. We define our universe as the totality of all things which are within the grasp of the human mind. But is one river an adequate metaphor for that kind of universe? Is there only one ever-deepening course for that full creative thrust of planets and galaxies to flow through?

---

*Notes appear at the end of each chapter.

Life has progressed through incessant groping and has experimented with many combinations. Most have yielded false starts and blind alleys; some, like most of our present colleagues on the earth, have been brilliant successes. Once a successful combination was found, it burst forth filling all the space it could reach and utilize. Combinations that arrived late and those which were unfit did not flourish and disappeared from the earth. Many other combinations might have occurred which could have been successful but it was too late, as their day had passed. The Mendelian mechanism of inheritance is much more efficient than it needs to be, having a potentiality far exceeding the opportunity. Theodosius Dobzhansky in his book *The Biology of Ultimate Concern* comments on this point: "A vast majority of potentially possible genetic endowments will never be realized . . . only a minuscule fraction of the possible gene combinations can ever be actualized."[3] Just consider the countless creatures which have never had the chance to emerge from the realm of the possible — the mutations whose time will never come and the variations of fin, foot, and wing which have never been tried out on the earth.

Thus, the biological world as it develops on the earth is poignantly incomplete. There is neither time nor space enough on the earth for all possibilities to be explored. The opportunities available ten million years ago when paths leading toward *Homo sapiens* were being explored no longer exist. Many such evolutionary paths will forever remain untrodden and unexplored. Certain routes were taken due to environmental challenges. With a different set of challenges than those present on the continent of Africa a few million years ago, we cannot guess what other gene combinations would be propagating themselves across the earth of the twentieth century.

Is it possible that the universe is as incomplete as life on the earth? Can the universe be similar to the biosphere of the earth: incredibly complex but incomplete, containing only a few of the vast number of possible forms of reality? Of course there may be life elsewhere in the universe, and those experiments which have not been attempted on our planet may be flourishing in the far-flung reaches of a galaxy we can only dimly see in our sky. It is therefore possible that in the billions of planets in the universe on which life may be developing, evolution of the scale of the universe may not be left incomplete. However, since there is but one universe, everything that is to be accomplished must be accomplished here.

So we return to the peculiar question of our universe. In its aloneness, is it *complete* and *unique*? Perhaps there are other equally effective ways of combining energy and matter which could result in universes, physical laws, and forces completely unrecognizable to us. If such other alien architectures are possible but never created, how was our particular universe chosen? Could it be that we are the outcome of one fearful toss of dice — just one of innumerable possible outcomes, each of which represented completely independent universes? Perhaps a gathering of matter and energy, bizarre beyond imagination, was almost projected into reality while one of the dice of that awesome game landed on an edge and teetered indecisively between two independent universes, neither of which contradicted or duplicated the other. Finally, the motion of the dice was stilled and our universe became. That strange, unrealized, now forever forbidden construction of energy and matter remains on the other side of reality, in the words of T.S. Eliot in "Burnt Norton":

> . . . an abstraction
> Remaining a perpetual possibility
> Only in a world of speculation.[4]

If we sense that something is missing in our universe — that a symmetry is left incomplete or a process is remaining unfulfilled — we may be reaching for what is not nor ever shall be. In our search for a particularly elusive elementary particle or a predicted but undiscovered star, we may be seeking a phenomenon that is contained in other universes on those other faces of the dice which we shall never see.

In his book *Flatland*, Abbott describes an incomplete world: a society of two-dimensional creatures imprisoned on a two-dimensional surface.[5] For them the third dimension, height, was utterly inconceivable. The other dimensions were totally inaccessible to them as they scurried around in their two dimensions. At the edge of their surface was another universe closed to them and their descendants for eternity. It is possible that in the future, man similarly imprisoned on the surface of his dice — his chance but incomplete universe — will wander to the edge and encounter a looming, dumb darkness in which variety and surprises peter out: that other universe inaccessible and nonexistent.

> Footfalls echo in the memory
> Down the passage which we did not take
> Towards the door we never opened . . .[6]

The vision of such a finite future for mankind is unsettling. It is one matter to be a human being who can toss dice, but it is quite another to have our entire reality the consequence of one single toss. The vitality and fullness of the universe may be only a thin facade overlying the bounded and limited results of just one outcome of a game of chance. We hope that our reality is more than the repetitive strain of a broken phonograph record or the futureless stability of an ant colony.

The Richness of the Universe

Actually, the experiences of contemporary science tend to repudiate the suggestion of an incomplete and accidental universe: it is just too luxuriant. We link the facts of our world by means of metaphorical relationships which we call physical laws. There are an unlimited number of such metaphors, and we choose the simplest. Using this metaphorical linkage of facts as our guide we explore the world and we always discover new lands and strange phenomena. It is our experience in physics that few combinations of matter and energy which do not contradict our laws are absent from the universe. We examine our theory and note that a certain kind of particle is not prohibited. We search for it, and almost always it is there. Neutrinos, neutron stars, and the black hole have been discovered by such direct searching. Why the universe should be complete as judged by our simple metaphors is one of the great mysteries of modern science.

This sense of the completeness of the universe is contained in a principle first developed in an unusual way by the British novelist T.H. White in his classic *The Once and Future King*.[7] In the story the young King Arthur, known as Wart, has been in bed for three days with a broken collarbone following a successful battle with a griffin. Extremely bored by his enforced confinement, Wart appealed to his tutor, the magician Merlyn, to turn him into an ant so that he might explore a glass-enclosed ant farm in his room. With some reluctance Merlyn consented to the persistent requests of the invalid, and Wart suddenly found himself, antennae and all, standing in a boulder-strewn field outside an ant fortress. Above each tunnel leading into the fortress was written the notice: Everything Not Forbidden is Compulsory. Known by some as the "totalitarian principle of physics," White's principle has recently been invoked by physicists to justify searches for undiscovered yet not forbidden particles, such as the faster-than-light tachyon.

To conclude our story, Wart found the Orwellian world of ants, with the queen playing the role of "big brother," extremely disagreeable. Continuous activity was compulsory, and there was always a voice in his head making certain that his only effort was for the good of the nest. Just before becoming involved in a pointless war with a neighboring nest, he was returned to his bed by Merlyn.

What a strange and unlikely place to initially encounter such a magical idea as the complete universe! If the principle does apply to our universe, it is anything but totalitarian in its freedom and promise. It speaks of a marriage of uniformity and infinity, of order and freedom, of boundaries and boundlessness which mankind has barely started to explore. There is an undeniable order and lawfulness in our universe; yet that order may be enriched by an infinity of diversity which does not contradict that order. In leaving nothing incomplete and no possibility unexpressed, the cosmos swells beyond the power of our metaphor. Can one, for instance, imagine a continuum of rivers, of which our river is but one of an infinite number of possible forms?

Perhaps our idea of the complete universe can be illuminated by the comparison of a violin and a piano. The piano does not produce a continuum of notes; it can generate only a series of successive and distinct tones which are separated from each other by gaps and do not meld. The violin, on the other hand, is capable of producing a series of continuous tones, far more, of course, than can be separated by the human ear. Since no laws prohibit the playing of these intermediate tones and since the tones are always available for touch of the bow or pluck of the finger, the violin or the human voice is a closer analogy to the complete continuum of the universe than is the piano.

We expect a rich repertory for the voice and violin, and not surprisingly we have been encountering an increasingly rich repertory of the continuous universe. During the 1960s there was an unfolding of extraordinary riches in the astronomical universe as part of its continuum was explored. A series of largely unanticipated wonders have become visible: exploding galaxies, quasars, interstellar bio-clouds, light from the fireball of creation, and neutron stars. These discoveries increase the extravagant variety of the universe of which we are already well aware: dolphins, neutrinos, clusters of galaxies, dragon flies, redwoods, comets, and sunspots. There have been strong hints of even greater mysteries awaiting exploration: anti-galaxies, white holes, worm holes, quarks, tachyons, and many other "things that go bump in the night." The world that we experience is rich and is becoming richer at every glance. Thus far we have experienced no attenuation of these surprises and subtleties of nature as we improve our ability to make closer contact with the universe.

The improvement of our senses has proven to be crucial in determining our ability to survey the mysteries of the universe. We possess extraordinarily complex organs of sense perception: eyes, fingers, skin, ears, nose, tongue. They are designed, however, for creatures living on a very particular rock which is in orbit around a particular star. Our eyes are designed specifically for a landscape illuminated by that star, our sun. The color sensitivity, of the human eye is an almost exact duplicate of the color distribution of the energy of the sun: the sun is brightest in the yellow-green near a wavelength of 5000 Angstroms($\mathring{A}$), and our eyes are most sensitive near 5000 $\mathring{A}$. Our heritage is certain: we are children of our star.

As a consequence, we look out at the universe through an incredibly small window. Our eyes are sensitive to wavelengths lying between 3000 $\mathring{A}$ and 6600 $\mathring{A}$. (One $\mathring{A}$ is 100-millionth of a centimeter, 10^{-8} cm, and an even smaller fraction of a kilometer, 10^{-13} km.) However, the technology of the twentieth century has built more powerful eyeglasses, or detectors, and we have been able to measure x-rays and gamma rays coming from outside the earth with wavelengths less than 1 $\mathring{A}$. At the opposite end of the

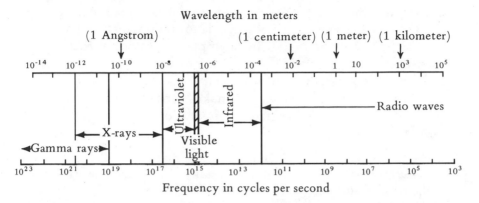

Figure 2-1. The electromagnetic spectrum. Note the very narrow window of visible light.

spectrum of electromagnetic radiation, radio waves from the sun have been detected with wavelengths greater than a kilometer.

Unaided, our eyes can thus sense approximately 10^{-10} or one 10-billionth of the full range of the electromagnetic spectrum which we have detected by artificial means (Figure 2-1). One 10-billionth is a small number, and a slice of pumpkin pie which is that fraction of the full pie would yield very little nourishment. For instance, a crystal of salt that could fit through the holes of a saltshaker seen at a distance of 100 miles would appear as large as the end of that slice of pie seen from its tip. Yet consider the degree to which we rely upon our eyes to guide us in our modeling of the world. It is truly incredible that the picture of the world we have composed by means of our nonvisual senses bears any resemblance to that which we perceive through our eyes. For instance, the most recent observations using radio waves and x-rays have essentially confirmed the general details of the model of the universe we built from our visual images. Our extrapolations were remarkably valid.

Our experience is not unlike that of creatures living on a planet surrounded by an opaque shell which prevents all light of the outside world from reaching them except through a small hole punctured in the shell, the same size as the hole of a saltshaker at a distance of 100 miles. It was by means of such limited information that we tried to piece together the nature of the outside world before the twentieth century. Now, of course, the universe is better lighted. In spite of the great gulf which lies between what can be known of the universe and what our still-limited perceptual abilities enable us to know, we are able to compose, albeit haltingly, a picture of the universe. In most places it is out of focus, the color balance is poor, and there are large blank areas, but we can make out the suggestions of dim shapes and forms. That we are able to see anything at all which makes sense reminds us of the amazement of Ivan Karamazov speaking of a slightly different sort of gulf.

> What is strange, what is marvelous, is not that God really exists; the marvel is that such an idea of the necessity of God could have entered the head of such a savage and vicious beast as man; so holy it is, so moving, so wise, and such a great honor it does to man.[8]

It is a great honor to man that he is able to be receptive to the unfamiliarity of the universe — that he is able to accept with honesty those aspects of the world which violate his preconceived notions. A person who has always lived in a room illuminated only by faint red light may do one of two things when the room is suddenly flooded with white light. He may retreat to a corner, close his eyes, and refuse to accept the unfamiliar. Or he may look carefully at the light and discover that the white light does not contradict or invalidate his previous red light. Then he may use the newly acquired power of the white light to learn more about his room. The fact that he has chosen to follow the latter course indeed does him great honor.

There is reward for such an enhanced awareness; something is to be seen in that room filled with white light, and it awaits to be experienced and explored. Moreover, once a new phenomenon has been sighted in the depths of space, we frequently have the haunting feeling that we have seen it somewhere before — that it has been woven all along into the tapestry of our world. In the past we saw only portions of that pattern which can now be recognized in greater detail. These astronomical surprises such as quasars and pulsars are thus not unrelated to us in the sense that heaven and earth were separated by Aristotle. They partake of the same metaphors which unite our local experiences. As we discover new features of the universe we discover new and more complex interrelationships. It is as though we are digging in a forest and encounter at deeper and deeper levels a web of tightly interwoven roots. The deeper we dig, the more tangled the mass of roots becomes and the more difficult it is to separate individual root systems. We may wrestle with the tangle of roots and become ever more frustrated in our attempts to identify the roots of a single tree which seems to get submerged in a suffocating complexity. Eventually we may cease fighting the tangle and consider the complex mixture of roots and trees. Then we find that seemingly unrelated complexities are unified by a small number of rules and concepts. In a similar fashion, we are currently operating in the physical sciences with an amazingly small number of laws and metaphors. The universe has exercised beautiful restraint in its law making.

We are not participating in a game for which new rules must be invented each time new situations are encountered (although the old rules will undoubtedly be replaced as entirely new realms of experience become available to us). What we are discovering is that the universe has been constructed so skillfully that only a few carefully worded statements are necessary to describe the majority of the known phenomena of the universe. We judge the effectiveness of these statements not only by their consistency with experience but also by their inherent simplicity. As our perception is sharpened by means of electron microscopes and x-ray telescopes, we become more skillful in detecting the simplicity underlying diversity. It is the marvelous paradox of modern science that simplicity and complexity grow together. As we experience and enjoy more of the complexity of the universe, we perceive more of its essential wholeness. The universe becomes more lean as we immerse ourselves in its richness.

We reach into space and find ourselves returning to the descriptions we have composed for our local environment; we marvel that such descriptions could include so many phenomena which we had not predicted or imagined. Indeed, one of the extraordinary accomplishments of science is the systematic demonstration of the consistency of the universe. It is remarkable that the same set of laws we have established to describe our spinning experiences on earth applies equally well to the spinning pulsar deep in the center of the Crab nebula more than 3000 light-years away from us. By means of our physics one can reconcile the sound produced as a bow is drawn across the string of a violin with the sound of an alien star.

If the pulsar is consistent with the sound of the violin, how many more yet undiscovered, bizarre creations may exist which similarly do not violate our terrestrial physics? How many more sounds may lie between the familiar notes? How many more branches of the tree of evolution may exist somewhere in the galaxy because they are not prohibited by our small collection of laws? If the universe is complete, then all of these noncontradictory opportunities must exist beyond our solar system in numbers and variety that stagger the imagination.

Black Clouds, Neutrinos, and Pulsars

The belief that whatever is possible must exist somewhere in the universe is the essence of science fiction, which at its best is an exploration of the possibilities existing in the universe which do not contradict the laws of nature as we now understand them. It is, of course, pleasantly ironical that successful science fiction at its prophetic best ceases to be fiction after some time.

Much of what is occurring at the growing tips of science today may be described also as good science fiction. Especially in astrophysics there is much speculative and very playful theorizing which is offered in the same spirit as science fiction: the exploration of the noncontradictory possibilities of the universe. In the case of scientific theorizing there is a very crucial constraint placed upon the exploration of noncontradictions in that the possibility of disproving the speculations must be built into the theory. Science demands communication between the world of sensory experiences and the world of imagination. There must be frequent cross talk and feedback between these two worlds. The most skillfully constructed scientific theory is the most fragile because it has built into it predictions which may unambiguously test its validity. Even after such a theory has been disproved, it may be admired for its beauty but not for its truth. Science fiction, in contrast, has the freedom to explore beyond this realm wherein scientific theory operates. However, neither good science nor good science fiction can afford to be loose with the facts. Both must conform to the collection of experiences we have acquired in the physical world and then project into the world beyond.

Figure 2-2. The Crab nebula photographed in red light. The location of the neutron star is shown by the arrow. (Lick Observatory.)

When the astronomer Fred Hoyle speculated about the steady-state universe, the perfect cosmological principle, and the process of continuous creation, he and his colleagues clearly stated how their theory could be disproved by means of straightforward observations of the astronomical universe. And indeed, based on observations of the past few years, the theory of the steady-state universe appears to have passed into the realm of beautiful but disproven theories. On the other hand, when Hoyle wrote science fiction and speculated in *The Black Cloud*[9] about an intelligent and communicative interstellar dust cloud, he offered no such specific test which could challenge his ideas. It is ironical that the black cloud may be more of a reality than the steady-state universe. Recent observations at radio frequencies have identified complex organic molecules such as formic acid and formaldehyde in interstellar dust clouds, thereby adding credence to his suggestion that highly complex organizations of molecules may occur in the many clouds of gas and dust lying between the stars. In both his science and science fiction, Hoyle was exploring with a great deal

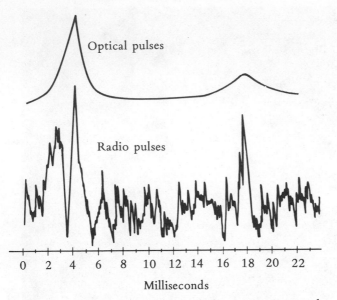

Figure 2-3. Optical and radio "light curves," signals from the Crab nebula. The ragged appearance of the radio curve results principally from the irregular effects of the interstellar medium on propagating radio waves. (From Louis Berman, *Exploring the Cosmos*, p. 320. Copyright © by Little, Brown and Company (Inc.). Reprinted by permission.)

of imagination and talent the freedoms inherent in current physics and astrophysics.

In the 1930s J. Robert Oppenheimer and a number of other physicists began in a similar spirit to explore the freedoms available in the structure and behavior of matter at very high pressure. They concluded that beyond a certain pressure an atom would crumble like an eggshell and the electrons would be absorbed into the central nucleus. The result would be a gas of closely packed neutrons. An ordinary star, they theorized, might become unstable and collapse inward to produce a droplet of neutron gas a mere 10 or 20 kilometers in diameter. To this imaginary giant nucleus which would have the mass of 10^{56} or 10^{57} ordinary nuclei, they gave the name *neutron star.* Nothing at that time appeared to forbid the formation of such a superdense neutron star, but for thirty years it remained an intriguing possibility which no one was able to detect.

Then one finally emerged in the entirely unexpected shape of a pulsar. In 1967 at the University of Cambridge, a series of radio pulses were detected which seemed to originate from outside the earth. The British radio astronomers had serendipitously stumbled on a neutron star. The pulses, still continuing, are apparently being produced by a rapidly spinning neutron star, the remnant of a supernova explosion in which a large star almost destroyed itself. Since the detection of the first pulsar, more than 140 have been discovered; the presence of neutron stars in our galaxy appears to be well established. The fastest spinning neutron star lies in the center of the Crab nebula, the remnant of the supernova of 1054 A.D. (Figures 2-2 and 2-3).

It should be noted that these pulsars are more than mere oddities which are afraid to disturb the universe, measuring out their balding lives with meaningless pulses. Rather, they appear to play a preeminent role in the origin of one of the great enigmas of the galaxy: the rain of cosmic rays constantly falling on the earth. It appears that cosmic rays, which are protons traveling at speeds close to that of light, may be accelerated by the swinging magnetic arms of these swiftly spinning neutron stars.

The story of the detection of a neutron star is closely related to the discovery of the neutrino. This particle was proposed in an almost tongue-in-cheek fashion by Wolfgang Pauli in 1930 as an attempt to lessen the embarrassment of physicists in connection with the process of beta decay. In this process of nuclear metamorphosis, a neutron transforms itself into (or replaces itself by) a proton, and an electron is ejected by the neutron in the process. The curious and unsettling aspect was that the electron moved away from the neutron with an unpredictable speed: sometimes quickly, sometimes slowly. This variability in speed meant that a variable amount of energy was apparently required to transform the neutron into the proton. Yet a proton with identical characteristics resulted each time regardless of the speed or energy of the ejected electron. It was hence impossible to account for all the energy involved in beta decay, as it appeared that some was leaking away in an unpredictable fashion.

The concept of energy conservation is a venerable and useful tool in physics, allowing a great simplification of apparently complex phenomena. Before this embarrassment of beta decay was recognized, one always could add the energies distributed among various particles at the beginning of a process and look forward to finding the same total energy at the end. Pauli felt that the idea of energy conservation was worth saving, and he attempted to plug the leak by postulating that another particle, unobserved at that time, was carrying away a variable amount of energy. The sum of the energies of the electron and the new particle should then always be constant, allowing a balancing of the energies on both sides of the process. Nothing seemed to forbid the presence of such a particle, so why shouldn't there be one? A few years later the idea was developed in detail by Enrico Fermi, who named the still un-observed particle a *neutrino*.

The neutrino remained only a fascinating and useful possibility for many more years than Pauli or Fermi would have liked. It was frequently explained by physicists to their friends with an embarrassed snicker; it saved appearances; and it was not forbidden by any known rule. But did the universe really contain it? Finally in 1956, after five years of effort, Clyde Cowan and Frederick Reines succeeded in identifying the neutrino in a stream of particles emanating from the Savannah River nuclear reactor.

Now it appears that the universe is being filled with these elusive particles which pour out of the interiors of stars in vast swarms. Because they represent so much lost and irretrievable energy they establish more firmly than anything else the direction of the arrow of time. They make indelible the writing of the moving hand of the *Rubaiyat*.

Other Universes/Other Realities

Encouraged by the fact that Einstein's general theory of relativity does not forbid fields of gravity so strong that light cannot escape, black holes were sought. It was postulated that if a large star could collapse to an object only a few miles in diameter, it would permanently trap with its gravity all matter and energy which ventured too close. Since there may be many such collapsed objects in our galaxy, a black hole hunt appeared to have a good chance of success. The hunt has apparently been successful for there seems to be a black hole swinging around a star in the constellation of Cygnus. Matter appears to have been torn away from the hole's

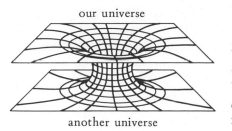

our universe

another universe

Figure 2-4. The Einstein-Rosen bridge connecting two flat universes. (After Figure 7-3 "The Wormhole" (p. 55) from *Relativity and Cosmology* by William J. Kaufmann, III, Harper & Row, 1973.)

companion, and as it plunges into the black hole it emits bursts of x-rays which have been detected.

Other realms, which only writers of science fiction have dared dream about, may be made accessible by the black hole. As it falls out of our universe into the black hole, matter may pass into other universes. The distortion of space-time produced by the collapsed star may connect us to many universes through a tunnel known as the *Einstein-Rosen bridge* (Figure 2-4). As matter falls into a black hole, it experiences increasingly curved space-time. Eventually, however, according to the calculations of Einstein and Rosen, the curvature of space-time decreases and the matter emerges into another universe. If the hole is sufficiently large such that one is not torn apart by the intense gravity at its edge, a black hole may provide an entrance for the adventuresome traveler to innumerable other realities. Even today we may be visited by objects from other universes, for it has been speculated that the bright centers of quasars may be black holes in reverse through which matter is pouring from elsewhere.

Will the universe ever grow faded and stagnant? Will our feet ever come to rest securely on the solid bottom of ultimate reality in touch with the absolute laws of physics such that new phenomena will never again suddenly appear to surprise us? Probably not, answers the physicist David Bohm in his book *Causality and Chance in Modern Physics*.[10] There may be no such items in our universe as final and absolute laws. The most recent deluge of new phenomena in physics and astronomy suggests no surrender by the universe in her ability to create qualitatively new forms. Call her Scheherazade, as her ingenuity is inexhaustible.

Bohm asserts that our most sacred laws of physics will eventually prove to be inadequate. Such has always been the fate of old laws. Each was merely a ledge providing a temporary foothold for our progress up the cliff. There may be an infinity of such footholds, each qualitatively different from all the others and all leading upward across the cliff which has no end.

A dizzying possibility, this infinity of the cosmos! It is much like the glance down the stairwell of a high building as one becomes aware of the spiraling space that lies underneath. Below the present layer of this onion-skinned reality of ours lies another layer, and beneath it there are infinitely more layers, each containing new experiences and perhaps new physical laws.

We thus find ourselves sitting down to an extraordinary feast. The scientific laws and theories that we have created to unite our current facts may be just a few of the infinite number of ways they could be related. The laws that we have chosen, based upon the criterion of simplicity, should not be unique, for simplicity was judged on the basis of human experience. If there is no limit to the number of independent and nonduplicating ways of describing our universe, each particular description must be infinitely incomplete. The mystery in which we live is thus not so much the size and richness of our world, but it is the seemingly unwarranted success that we, living in an infinitesimal portion of it, have managed to achieve. Bertrand Russell has commented on this enigma: "We know very little, and yet it is astonishing that so little knowledge can give us so much power."

In *The Unexpected Universe*, Loren Eiseley repeats a friend's remark which touches upon our speculations of undiscovered realities interpenetrating and underlying our present reality. During a performance of an opera in a tent at Cape Cod, they watched a moth fly past the bright arc lights moving amongst the music which filled the tent. "He doesn't know," his friend commented. "He's passing through an alien universe brightly lit but invisible to him. He's in another play; he doesn't see us. He doesn't know. Maybe it's happening to us. Where are we? Whose is the real play?"[11]

The universe in its completeness has room enough for many moths and for many plays.

NOTES

1. Herman Hesse, *Siddhartha* (New York: New Directions, 1951), p. 83.

2. Herman Hesse, op. cit., p. 110.

3. Theodosius Dobzhansky, *The Biology of Ultimate Concern* (New York: World, 1969), p. 125.

4. T.S. Eliot, "Burnt Norton," in *The Complete Poems and Plays, 1909-1950* (New York: Harcourt, Brace, 1952), p. 117.

5. Edwin A. Abbott, *Flatland* (New York: Dover, 1952).

6. T.S. Eliot, loc. cit.

7. T.H. White, "The Sword in the Stone," in *The Once and Future King* (New York: Berkley, 1966), p. 122.

8. Fyodor Dostoevsky, *The Brothers Karamazov* (New York: Random House, Modern Library, 1950; originally published 1880), p. 279.

9. Fred Hoyle, *The Black Cloud* (New York: Harper and Row, 1952).

10. David Bohm, *Causality and Chance in Modern Physics* (Philadelphia: University of Pennsylvania Press, 1957), ch. V.

11. Loren Eiseley, *The Unexpected Universe* (New York: Harcourt, Brace, & World, 1969), pp. 175-176.

'Truth *is simply the complete coherence of the universe in relation to every point contained within it. Why should we be suspicious of or underestimate this coherence just because we ourselves are the observers? We hear continually of some sort of anthropocentric illusion contrasted with some sort of objective reality. In fact, there is no such distinction. Man's truth is the truth of the universe for man: in other words it is simply truth.'* ('Esquisse d'un univers personnel', 4 May 1936)

Père Teilhard de Chardin, 1936

L'energie humaine, Paris: Seuil, 1962, quoted in J. Mortier and M. Auboux, *The Teilhard de Chardin Album*, New York: Harper and Row, 1966.

Chapter Three

Science: Our Modern Mythology

The Similarity of Myth and Science

Myths are public dreams, suggests Joseph Campbell,[1] in which the illuminations of the dream are expressed in ways which are valid for all mankind. So too is our science a collection of dreams made public by the language of mathematics and shared concepts. These earth dreams, born of creatures who have slept on the surface of one particular planet and written in terrestrial words and symbols, are means for humanizing the cosmos.

The universe and its collection of phenomena need to be made familiar, and our cosmological myths have always been attempts to provide mankind with a comfortable and familiar home. The sequence of cosmic models starting with an earthy disc floating on a cosmic ocean underneath a clamshell sky, through the rotating crystalline spheres and the swinging epicycles, to the present big-bang cosmology, have all been attempts to make the universe small enough to place within our reach. When one is living in a large, darkened hall, how much more comforting it is to build partitions which one can see and feel and to hang surrogate windows on the wall, remaking the darkness outside into familiar scenes!

Without a ruling mythology, the world remains chaotic and fragmentary — a series of unrelated images, moving in from and out to the surrounding darkness. Those old cosmologies survived only while they fulfilled their roles of providing secure walls and giving useful advice for dealing with future experiences. Without the continuity provided by our myths and science, human memory would be an overcrowded warehouse filled with fact piled upon fact, each useless because no fact would ever be connected with another. The capriciousness of the natural world is decreased by the predictive powers of myth and science, and as a result the most effective course of action can be chosen from a number of possible alternatives.

Not only do they provide guidance for future activity, but science and myth also establish criteria for appropriate and effective behavior in the present. In science the acceptable mode of behavior is established by what Thomas Kuhn describes as the *paradigm* of science.[2] With a function very similar to that of a set of social mores, the paradigm of science establishes suitable areas and acceptable styles of research, proper tests for validity of a theory, and standards of ethical behavior. Without such a tradition the scientist would frequently find it difficult to know what would be a useful experiment to perform and to be able to communicate the results of that experiment in an unambiguous manner. Mark Schorer notes a similar interdependency between mythology and literature: ". . . literature would be impossible without a previous imaginative consent to a ruling mythology."[3]

Myth and science also provide a language for communicating new ideas, allowing an individual to bring into the light of day his dreams of the morning. Human fantasy needs a medium in which it can be shared as, for instance, Einstein's strong sense of the unity of the world found expression in the language of physics. He was able to share his intuition only because a suitable language existed and because he knew how to express it in a manner which was acceptable to the other members of his scientific culture.

Jung notes that ordinary human speech plays the same role of determining which of one's innermost thoughts can be communicated: "Speech is a storehouse of images founded in experience, and therefore concepts which are too abstract do not easily take root, or quickly die out again for lack of contact with reality."[4] One does not need to go far to discover experiences which are too abstract for western science to handle. Unidentified flying objects, clairvoyance, human auras, and telepathy are all examples of experiences which have not taken root in the scientific establishment. The ideas of general relativity are no less abrasive to our everyday consciousness, but they have been expressed in the language of science, have been found credible, and therefore have flourished.

Myth is always difficult to identify from the inside, and because of the quality of the falseness that we frequently associate with it, we often find it difficult to admit that modern science is a myth. However, when one is living and participating in a mythology, it has the full authority of truth even to the extent that men are willing to fight and die in its name. Unlike folk tales such as *Cinderella* and *Snow White*, myth can evoke intense commitment and total belief in its truthfulness. Likewise we believe in our science and are continuously placing ourselves at its mercy. Our level of trust is indeed extraordinary as, for instance, whenever we step into a jet aircraft, encourage the astronauts to fly to the moon, or allow medical science to work upon our bodies. But no scientist will ever claim that his science is completely free of error.

Indeed, the most compelling similarity between science and myth is the drama each derives from living in that twilight zone between fantasy and reality. Physics lives there just as assuredly as do the ancient stories of gods and goddesses and demons, for physics is never unrestrictedly true. It is only temporarily true, and in a broader context it is always false for sometime in the future each of our theories will most likely be disproved by a new discovery. Yet physics has the compelling appearance of truth: human sounds are carried by a wireless, men land on the moon, energy emerges from the atom. Neither science nor mythology has more claim to truth, as each is but a link between the inner world of man's imagination and the outer world of physical reality. This mythological dimension of physics is recognized in the amazement of Dirac or Einstein that their search for beauty and simplicity in the inner world of abstract mathematics should find application in the outer physical world. In both there is that delicate blending of the inner vision and the outer world which must be "neither too good or too bad to be true nor too true."[5] Science which would be *too* true would not be science, but a catalogue of facts, a listing of the wind speed, the temperature, or the people seen on a particular day. The power of modern science is derived from the metaphorical linkage between facts, not from the facts by themselves.

Thus science, the actor, emerges from the darkened wings of the human mind into the bright lights of shared experience, pretending in spite of the mask and the costume that he is real, his world is real, and that he is more than an actor. Yet all the time he knows that he is only pretending and that he will be judged not by the quality of his truth but by the quality of his illusion. Truth slips from our hands when we insist that science be true.

The old myths succeeded in evoking an extraordinary variety of human response. They were always available to focus and release human energy for a mixture of purposes, ranging from the destructiveness of war to the creativeness of art. Today in the austere costume of science, the symbols still perform their magic but only for those few who can read the symbolic language. Late in life while he was still struggling with his unified field theory, Einstein wrote to a friend: "I cannot tear myself away from my work. It has me inexorably in its clutches." This extraordinary man was participating in a drama which was for him no less intense, no less captivating than the great celebrations of our planet. If we could realize that these symbols of science — as old as mankind — have merely been reworked and reinterpreted in the modern style, each of us could touch and recapture some of the excitement and mystery of the world where myths are real, masks are the face, and science is pure, joyful fantasy.

Recycling the Old Symbols

Our heritage of old myths contains more than quaint and awkward explanations of phenomena — explanations which have been corrected by our present scientific laws and discoveries. The early myths are part of the continuous recycling of human symbols which people at various times have used to communicate their intuitions about the nature of man and his world. Many of the old symbols such as the atomicity of matter and unity of nature have not been crushed and discarded. Instead, they have decomposed into compost to fertilize the imaginations of the physicist, poet, and playwright and to assist them in their business of humanizing the newer world. Chogyam Trungpa in his book *Meditation in Action* describes this process of recycling the old symbols and concepts.

It is said . . . that unskilled farmers throw away their rubbish and buy manure from other farmers, but those who are skilled go on collecting their own rubbish, in spite of the bad smell and unclean work, and when it is ready to be used they spread it on their land, and out of this they grow their crops. . . . Through thousands and thousands of lives we have been collecting so much rubbish that now we have a wonderful wealth of this manure. It has everything in it so it would be just the right thing to use, and it would be such a shame to throw it away. *Because if you do throw it away . . . all that struggle and all that collecting would have been wasted and you would have to start all over again from the beginning.*[6] (italics added)

Physics refers to this practice of sifting and preserving manure as the *correspondence principle,* suggested by Niels Bohr in the early 1900s when the old physics was being dismembered and rebuilt according to the new architecture of quantum mechanics. New and unfamiliar aspects of the world were being recognized which seemed incompatible with the ordinary world. However, the experiences of the past still had to be valid; they could not be ignored. Bohr suggested in his correspondence principle that the old experiences could be used to test the new synthesis. The description of an electron contained within an atom must be sufficiently general so that as one comes increasingly close to the world of redwoods and turtles, the same description and the same equation can also describe the large-scale world. For instance, in our current model of the atom the electron closest to the nucleus has no resemblance to the common grapelike image we have of an electron; it is more like a diffuse cloud hanging about the center. However, in orbits much further from the nucleus the electron begins to look increasingly like a planet swinging around a star (although bound to the nucleus by an electrical force, not a gravitational force).

Thus, the carefully designed and documented experiences of the old physicists were not abandoned. The correspondence principle built a bridge between the old and new, between the familiar and the bizarre. Trungpa had, of course, a more profound relationship in mind than the correspondence between the small and large phenomena of the physical world. His metaphor of the field of manure applies to the entire field of human activity, and it is an enlarged version of the correspondence principle, combining ancient legends and new science, which we are interested in exploring in this book.

Western science did not spring fully developed into the modern world; rather, it has roots which reach deep into the childhood of our species. Today's science contains new insights which have been cultivated in the gardens of the twentieth century. To deny the youthfulness of some of our science would be to deny the growth and evolution of our culture. But the similarities to prior world views are sometimes just as profound as are the differences. The visions of science well up from that same deeply hidden source which nourishes music, literature, and art. To be able to recognize that similarity is to open oneself to an entirely new level of experiencing the universe.

Unity in Variety

The most influential symbol in western science is that of unity in variety. The faith that such unity can be perceived and experienced by mankind nourishes the scientist and mystic. Its quest may be interpreted as a human response to the ancient desire of mankind to find a harmony in nature which contains a place in it for our species. Since we have long been worried by the apparent separation of our species from the natural world, in culture after culture — primitive to the high civilizations — mythologies have attempted to establish and reaffirm the wholeness of existence. In spite of its unfamiliar ways and death-dealing powers, science is part of that continuing effort by mankind to demonstrate that harmony can exist between the individual and his universe.

Our search for unity in science must be in part the result of the imprinting upon us of the coherence of the world through which we move. It does not require the trained eye of the professional ecologist to recognize that a forest is all of one piece: an intricate, interlocking system of sunlight, wild grasses, thunder echoes in the canyons, animals, moss, and flowing water. Its coherence presses firmly upon us and works its way into our pores like a sentence which is repeated over and over again.

There is an insistence to the wholeness of nature which we cannot easily ignore. Consider that river of which we spoke earlier. For men living on its banks, the river provides persistent encouragement in the quest for unity underlying variety. It flows on ceaselessly. Living by its side, one falls asleep with the sound of moving water. Morning comes and the water is still moving, sounding, changing; yet the river remains. The water moves relentlessly over the rocks lying on the bottom leaving white-crested hills on its surface. Water moves into those hills and then out again, yet the hills remain. Similarly, all the waters of the earth move in one pattern to the sea. The creatures of the earth appear and die, yet the species remains. The sun dies and is reborn day after day, yet the earth remains warm and alive. And within all of this change and unchange there lies man, folded into the pattern which is ever flowing.

These experiences of the continuity of nature are deeply in-grained in our consciousness. Perhaps living on another world at a different time, man would not possess such an overwhelming sense of the rightness of unity. But we have been well trained by our earth and sun, and it is wholeness we seek. The ever-returning sun has become one of our most persistent symbols of continuity. We have been carried by this planet around that orange globe several million times, and in that circling we have become saturated with the sun as a centering symbol. The rising and set-ting of the sun provide order for our lives; flowers open and close at the sun's bidding and they follow the sun in its trek across the sky; plants grow and die with the sun. At a very profound level the sun is the ultimate source of all the growing, changing, and emotion that occurs on our planet. The sun's presence and its varied influence provide a persuasive symbol of order overlying variety and a justification for the grouping, as in metaphor, of ex-periences around a focus.

Gravity, like the sun, is another attribute of our environment which is necessary for our survival. It clusters us together with the materials we need. Providing the converging influence necessary for the development of life, it is thus another primordial image of that face of order and unity which lies hidden behind variety and chaos. The sun, gravity, the permanence of species of animals in spite of the never-ending death of individuals, the cyclic seasons of growth, the regularity of astronomical phenomena — all provide not only models but, more significantly, forces driving mankind to identify explicitly the order felt by intuition. People have been drawn to that search by the basic fascination of these processes and not the less by the awe associated with their implications.

Many of us who practice science may have been initially drawn into science by a curiosity about ultimates. At first it was a kind of scientific materialism which seduced us — a naïve and hopeful curiosity involving fundamental questions about what the world is really like. I think we were possessed by a belief that something exists "out there" with more stability and more significance than ourselves and about which we might learn if we asked the right questions. But for many scientists this search for a simplistic truth about the universe matures with time into a curiosity about whether the part can be reconciled with the whole. There is a gradual realization that the truth is not attainable and really is not that exciting of a quarry after all. Questions involving *why* or even *what* cannot be answered with perfection. Too many new, different phenomena are appearing to allow us to describe *now* in its entirety. So the initial question and desired answer are absorbed into a new style of curiosity about the unity of the world. Our journey becomes an exploration of the interconnections between our sensory experiences. It is our task to make those connections which have never before been made.

What we can do is wonder — wonder whether or not we will be able to show that our particular experience is consistent with the larger collection of man's experiences. Therein lies the real challenge of science today: the demonstration of the coherence of the world. The act of science becomes that of making a statement about the world with no interpretation and no editorializing — an effective, concise statement unencumbered by unnecessary embellishments. The daily efforts of the scientist become a ritualistic affirmation of the current weltanschauung which allows no unconnected pieces in our universe. The individual fact by itself is without excitement; it is the interlacing of the facts which is so exhilarating.

It is indeed an odd game that we play. If one particular observation can be accommodated too easily into our collection of prior experiences, then the act of reconciliation becomes trivial and of little inherent interest. But when we encounter that obdurate fact, such as the observation of a distant quasar which outshines whole galaxies, then the game increases in excitement as we strive to demonstrate that it does not violate the rest of the world. Instead of going to our chapels each sunrise and chanting "the world is one with the Lord," we perform the remarkably similar act of going to our telescopes or laboratories to affirm that the world is indeed one with itself.

Circles and Apples

It is also an old game — old apparently even when civilization appeared on the muddy plains of Sumeria around 3000 B.C. Man's first cities were built to be living expressions of the unity of the world. The ziggurat in the center of the city was the symbolic pivot of the universe, the motionless point of the spinning world. In the Etruscan cities the center, the *mundus*, was covered with a great stone called the soul stone, covering a deep shaft from which the spirits of the dead could rise. The city was transformed into a mini-cosmos through its circular shape. Thus, the circle has long been a symbol for the harmony of an ordered cosmos — the ultimate and perfect oneness of the universe and life. The rose windows of European cathedrals, the mandalas in Tibetan monasteries (Figure 3-1), and the ancient sun wheels engraved on neolithic rock walls all speak of the universal need of man to dip his finger into the basin of the world, and in rearranging it to create circular swirls in the plastic material of life.

In that primitive human circle of the round dance, the dancers create their own circular microcosm of one mind and one body. Unified as equal participants, with no beginning and no end and no leader and no followers, they repeatedly experience the timelessness of the circle. The circle moves but does not change. There is motion of the upraised and stamping feet, but no change or retreat: "There is only the dance." Submerged and dissolved into the symmetry of the perfect circle, they simply dance. Yet,

Figure 3-1. A Tibetan mandala, a symbolic representation of both the entire universe and the human body, i.e., the macrocosm and microcosm are of identical construction. The outermost circle represents the edge of the universe. Out of the core emanates energy and wisdom; the repetition of the ⊙ form signifies the interpenetration of the micro and macrocosm.

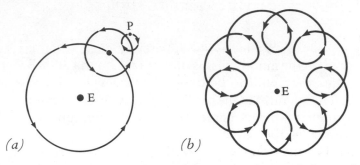

Figure 3-2. (a) Epicycles of Ptolemy. *(b)* An epicycle on a deferent showing eight retrograde loops of a planet.

"how can we know the dancer from the dance?"[7] Each is a complete representative of the whole. Because of its flawless symmetry, a dancer can know the circle by experiencing only one infinitesimal portion. Knowing just one spoke radiating from its center, he knows all spokes; dancing along one radius he dances all radii.

Inside the circle lies the center from which all parts are equally distant. Inside lies quietness, the focus which both attracts and repels. The center maintains the circle; it is the "... still point of the turning world. Neither flesh nor fleshless; neither from nor toward; at the still point, there the dance is."[8] In the perfection of the circle can be seen the face of the divine; in the stillness of its center lies the essence of the world; in its moving changelessness is eternity. Little wonder that man has long had a love affair with the circle! He seemingly cannot speak without circles bursting from his lips. Even the heavens have been remade by man in the image of a circle.

It is impossible to look at the Greek representations of the universe — the crystalline spheres of Aristotle and the circle upon circle of Ptolemy (Figure 3-2) — without saying to oneself, "Ah, yes! Here again is the hand of man searching for symbols to express the wholeness of the world." Indeed, for the Greeks the great challenge of astronomy was to demonstrate that the change, variety, and irregularity apparent in the sky could be refined into the order, elegance, and nonchange of circular patterns. The circle remained in the model of the solar system even in the sun-centered scheme proposed by Copernicus (Figure 3-3). Later, Kepler recognized that the orbits of the planets were not circles but

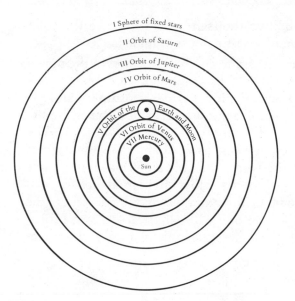

Figure 3-3. The Copernican universe, showing the circular orbits of the known astronomical objects in the fifteenth century.

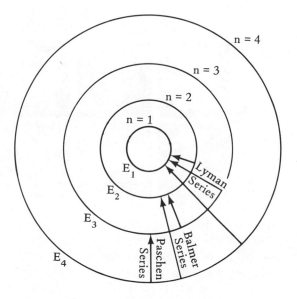

Figure 3-4. The Bohr atom, showing various electron orbits and transitions in hydrogen.

ellipses, and the effort of two thousand years to force the solar system into a circular mold was finally terminated.

Four centuries later, in 1913, the circle reappeared in the model of the atom with which Niels Bohr inaugurated man's new recognition of the world within. How very extraordinary and yet how natural that Bohr should use the ancient symbolism of the circle to represent his concept of the hydrogen atom (Figure 3-4). The marvelously adaptable circle was used again to communicate another intuition about the world. But the atom was not a circle and would not remain long forced into a circular shape. As with the solar system, the model of the atom was modified — this time by Arnold Sommerfeld — into one with elliptical electron orbits. Quantum mechanics has further refined our picture of the atom,

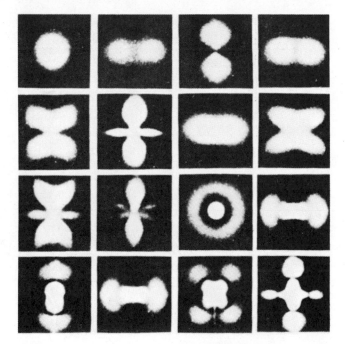

Figure 3-5.   Representations of the probability density of electron waves in atoms. The intensity of the shading corresponds approximately to the probability of finding an electron at that location in space. The circle is still present in today's atom but in a more subtle form. (Modified version of photograph from *Introduction to Atomic Spectra*, by H. E. White. Copyright © 1934 by McGraw-Hill, Inc. Used with permission of McGraw-Hill Book Co.)

and electrons are now represented by cloudlike waves which expand over the three-dimensional volume of the atom, bearing small resemblance to that original circle-mandala which started it all.

The law of gravity is one of mankind's most frequently used inventions and one of his most successful evocations of the unity of the world. It is a grand and ambitious metaphor encompassing fruit falling from terrestrial trees, moons circling planets, stars swinging in galaxies, and galaxies moving around each other in far-flung clusters of galaxies. Newton's synthesis is a merging of the local and the infinite, enabling us to gather in one glance that which adheres man and his associates to this world and connects his world with the rest of the universe.

The ingredients of his synthesizing vision were not unique to Newton. Many times before in other cultures models have been constructed using precisely the same items: fruit, the moon, man, and the earth. First, let us examine the circumstances surrounding Newton's synthesis.

In 1665 the Great Plague spread from London to Cambridge. College was dismissed and Isaac Newton, then 23 years old, moved to his mother's farm in Lincolnshire where he conducted experiments in chemistry and optics. One day as he sat in the garden, he watched an apple fall toward the earth. This observation led him to the following deduction:

> . . . I began to think of gravity extending to the orb of the Moon and having found out how to estimate the force with which a globe revolving within a sphere presses the surface of the sphere . . . I deduced that the forces which keep the Planets in their Orbs must be reciprocally as the squares of their distances from the centers about which they revolve; and thereby compared the force requisite to keep the Moon in her Orb with the force of gravity at the surface of the earth, and found them to answer pretty nearly. All this was in the plague years of 1665 and 1666 for in those days I was in the prime of my age for invention and minded Mathematicks and Philosophy more than at any time since.[9]

That the apple might be pulled to the earth by an invisible force was not Newton's contribution; such forces were postulated in the system of Aristotle. The unique and powerful attribute of Newton's vision was that the same force which pulls the apple also pulls the moon.

Many-faced gravity has remained silent as to why it should exist and why it should have these effects. That the ceremony of calculating inverse square force should work so successfully in providing a unity to the universe, remained a mystery which Newton could not penetrate. He wrote: "You sometimes speak of gravity as essential and inherent to Matter. Pray do not ascribe that Notion to me: for the cause of Gravity is what I do not pretend to know, and therefore would take more Time to Consider of it."[10] It is enough that it works. The Newtonian theory is a *description* of the world, not an explanation of it. "I frame no hypothesis," warned Newton; the apple falls and the moon swings, and he managed to find an appropriate method of describing both. Gravity remains as imponderable and inexplicable as much else surrounding us; it is "a good target for the poet," as Carl Sandburg would say.

Newton's route to his successful theory used the round moon as an indispensable ally. Indeed, how very contingent is his invention of gravity — contingent upon the presence of a moon circling the earth; upon the presence of only one sun in our solar system; and upon the absence of strong electrical and magnetic forces influencing the motion of the planets. If the planets had complex motions due to these other forces or due to the presence of two stars about which they orbited, it is very doubtful that Newton could have invented the simple idea of the force of gravity. Nor is it likely he would have created gravity were our planet barren of a satellite, as is Venus. The moon is 240,000 miles from the earth's center; the apple dangling from its branch is a mere 4000 miles from the center. Thus the moon is 60 times more distant from the center than is the apple. That difference enabled Newton to compare the force of gravity at two different locations. The moon is continually falling toward the earth just as the apple falls toward the earth. But the moon is a poor shot and invariably misses the earth, swinging past us in an elliptical orbit.

The moon does not accelerate as rapidly as the apple in its fall toward the earth. The apple accelerates 32 feet per second^2 as it leaves the branch of the tree. The moon, Newton was able to demonstrate, accelerates by an amount which is a factor of 60^2 smaller. The square of 60 is the square of ratio of the distance of the moon and apple from the center of the earth. And thus Newton

Figure 3-6. The metaphor of gravity: the apple, moon, man, and earth are tied together by Newton's invention.

proposed a "force of gravity" which had a strength inversely proportional to the square of the distance separating two bodies. Whether they be apples, moons, or people was immaterial; it was a democratic force acting equally on all pieces of the world.

That these independent aspects of the world should be related was and still is an awesome coincidence. Through the same sort of comparisons involving the planets orbiting the sun, Newton was able to show that in each case it appeared as if a force were acting upon all of the planets of the solar system which also decreased precisely as the square of the distance involved. It did not decrease as the cube of the distance for one planet and as the fourth power for another; it was always the square.

This was not an isolated coincidence. The moons of Jupiter form a miniature solar system, and for them it also appeared that they were drawn to Jupiter with a force which decreased inversely as the square of the distance. Today the list of such coincidences is lengthy, with examples reaching hundreds of millions of light-years away from Newton's home planet — far exceeding in their variety and subtleness what he could have imagined.

Across the world among the headhunting cannibals of New Guinea there is another metaphor involving fruit, the moon, and man. Rabia, one of the virgin dema, divinities "who appear in the ceremonies fabulously costumed to enact again the world-fashioning events of the 'time at the beginning of the world',"[11] was desired by the sun-man Tuwale as his wife. Her parents, disapproving of the match, placed a dead pig in her place in the wedding bed. Tuwale was understandably enraged at such deceit and proceeded to claim his bride by pulling her into the earth in a manner very reminiscent of the treatment of Persephone by Pluto. Her parents and friends were unable to prevent her from sinking deep among the roots of a tree. Finally when only her head remained above the ground, she called out to her mother and requested that she slaughter a pig and celebrate a feast, promising that three days later, in the evening, she, Rabia, would be in the sky shining as a new light. Indeed, her relatives, having done as she requested, looked to the east in the evening and saw the moon rising for the first time.

Death, killing, eating, and rebirth are all parts of the continuing cycle to which man is bound. And that ever-changing face of the moon is somehow inextricably intertwined with the life of man. Death was a prominent aspect of life for these headhunters of New Guinea who were also gardeners and planters. For them death and rebirth of the plant world had its undeniable counterpart in the world of man. Adolph Jensen gives the following description of the mythological synthesis of these people, which is extraordinary for its Newtonian overtones.

> Killing holds a place of paramount significance in the way of life both of animals and of men. Every day men must kill to maintain life. They kill animals, and apparently in the culture here being considered the

harvesting of plants was also regarded — quite correctly — as a killing.
. . . That killing should have assumed such a prominent position in the
total view of the world in their culture sphere, I should like to refer
quite specifically to the occupation of these people with the world of
plants. There was revealed to mankind in some measure a new field of
illumination. For the plants were continually being killed through the
gathering of their fruits, yet the death was extraordinarily quickly
overcome by their new life. *Thus there was made available to man a
synthesizing insight, relating his own destiny to that of the animals,
the plants, and the moon.*[12] (italics added)

Thus, the synthesis of a primitive, cannibalistic planting culture
with traditions extending back to the neolithic age brings together
the same ingredients as that of Newton. The excitement of this discovery does not come from any hint of a cause-effect relationship
between these synthesizing visions; Newton certainly did not
knowingly use this myth of Rabia as the starting point for his idea
of gravity. But he did use the same materials, and as a result of his
own unique point of view he arrived at a different conclusion.

The "Aha" Experience

What happened during those years of the plague in England was
very similar to a change in visual *gestalt*. The world itself had not
changed significantly between the birth of the myth of Rabia and
the birth of the idea of gravity. What changed was the rearranging
of the world in the perception of man. Something went "click" in
the mind of one man, and what had at one time seemed a
reasonable way of viewing the moon, an apple, and man was
replaced by a new pattern with new implications.

Gestalt refers to the act of perception in which an entire pattern
suddenly becomes evident. The experience is largely subjective
and is the antithesis of the laborious building-block approach
generally identified with science in which every minute detail is
scrutinized for a clue. In gestalt one's attention becomes focused
suddenly upon a particular figure standing out against a background. The interplay between figure and ground is sometimes
very dynamic. With different shifts of attention, the same ground
may give rise to different figures. Since the ground always changes
with time in the real world, it is hardly surprising that new gestalts

Figure 3-7. The reversible chalice. (From Howard H. Kendler, *Basic Psychology*, Third Edition. Copyright © 1974, W.A. Benjamin, Inc., Menlo Park, California.)

are constantly being formed. In the case of Isaac Newton, his gestalt occurred in 1666. Although it took him many years to work out the consequences, his crucial flash of insight must have come fairly quickly while he was sitting under the Lincolnshire apple tree. For him the interrelationship between earth, moon, and apple known as gravity was the "figure," and the world of the seventeenth century was the "ground."

A well-known example of the figure-ground effect in gestalt is the chalice which with an easy shift of attention becomes two heads seen in profile (Figure 3-7). Escher's woodcut "Heaven and Hell" is another example of figure-ground reversal in which there is competition between rival images (Figure 3-8). A somewhat more difficult switch of gestalt is found in the Schröder stairs: one can alternately "see" either the top or the bottom of the staircase (Figure 3-9). Note that no amount of detailed analysis of the lines in the drawing can accomplish or even facilitate the switch between the two perspectives. The switch occurs in some mysterious way in the mind of the beholder.

In the sketch "My Wife and My Mother-In-Law" by the cartoonist W.E. Hill, there exist two different ways of structuring the field: what was once a young woman in the eye of the viewer can become a mother-in-law. The same lines are there but they become gathered together in a different pattern. Here again one cannot

Figure 3-8. "Heaven and Hell," a woodcut by M.C. Escher, is an example of figure-ground reversal. (From the collection of C.V.S. Roosevelt, Washington, D.C.)

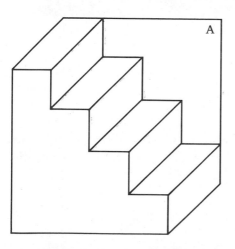

Figure 3-9. Schröder stairs, an example of perspective reversal.

Figure 3-10. "My Wife and My Mother-in-Law," by W.E. Hill.

reach the other pattern by analyzing the lines or scrutinizing it with a microscope. But once one has succeeded in structuring those lines in one's mind and perceiving the new pattern, it all seems so obvious.

In the case of both the Escher woodcut and Hill drawing, each competing pattern is capable of evoking opposite reaction in the viewer; contradictory patterns have been generated by the same lines. Is one pattern "wrong" and another "right"? Both are correct. Neither one by itself is the full story, just as no particular theory of physics is the full universe. Hill's picture is more than just the girl or just the mother-in-law and, of course, one of the morals of the Escher woodcut is that the world is neither entirely good nor entirely evil. What one sees is determined by where one's attention is directed.

For some people who have difficulty locating both of the ladies in Figure 3-10, the discovery of that face hidden among the lines comes as what the gestalt psychologists call an "aha" experience: the cascade of insights as a new way of perceiving the world becomes available. As a consequence we move into a more complex reality and have become more nimble in the process. We soon find it easy to shift from one pattern to another and then back again. Our previous world becomes enlarged, containing multiple patterns each of which is equally valid. Since there is no pressure for judgment, one has the freedom to switch back and forth at will, uncommitted to one arrangement or the other.

This "aha" experience is, of course, common in science; however, the old arrangements never seem as good or true. It is very difficult to remain uncommitted as we judge one pattern — Newtonian gravity, quantum mechanics, relativity — to be superior to another. Because of the extraordinary seductive quality of a synthesis such as that of Newton, we sometimes lose our nimbleness to move from one pattern to another. The exclusiveness of our science forces us to abandon a potential esthetic dimension of our world. We get trapped in one pattern because it appears to be "true" and fail thereby to experience the bittersweet sense in which both patterns may be partners in truth.

It is at this stage, when we cannot easily switch back to the old pattern, that a subtle change occurs in our science. The "as if" is dropped and the once tentative suggestion of a hypothesis becomes myth. Compare, for instance, two alternative statements of Newtonian gravity.

1. Two masses are drawn together as if there exists a force between them which varies inversely as the square of the distance. . . .
2. Between any two masses there exists a force of attraction which varies inversely as the square of the distance. . . .

The first is scientific hypothesis: a guess, a leap of the imagination. The second is myth: the mask has become the face. It seems to be a typical pattern for the guess of yesterday to become the myth of today when the "as if" is deleted unnoticed from the wording of the theory. It is dropped partly because it is cumbersome and partly because we assume our listeners realize they must add it for themselves. But also it is omitted because of the potential excitement of participating in a living myth — of moving fearlessly in that mythic structure without having to preface all of one's actions with "as if." The scientific theory remains symbolic and representative of experiences; it is certainly not the experience itself. Nor is it the only possible representation of the experiences for countless other potential gestalts remain to be perceived.

There seems little difference between investigating the innards of birds before launching ships toward Troy and scrutinizing the print-out of computers before sending rockets to the moon. Both rituals have acquired a certain credibility because of previous successes in our neighborhood of the universe, and both were associated with partial representations of experience. It might be argued that the Greeks relied upon divination only because they neglected to test their beliefs in a wide variety of situations; or perhaps they closed their minds to those instances in which these practices failed. The same charge can be leveled at Newtonian gravity. It works in some situations, but it appears satisfactory only if we neglect its shortcomings such as have been clearly identified by the general theory of relativity. Newtonian gravity is incorrect in its prediction for the advance of the perihelion of Mercury, for the bending of starlight near the sun, and for many other instances in which the pattern of general relativity appears superior to the pattern of gravity. But despite the limited applicability of the ritual of gravity, it still succeeds in certain situations. It still expresses the harmony, perceived only partially, which encloses us. In the partial realization of that harmony there comes a power not only to transform the individual but to transform the world.

One is again drawn to the recognition of the indispensability of man in science. The act of science is not merely that of a chemical reaction on a photographic plate — the mindless capture of what has already been present. The most influential acts have been of unique individuals eminently human in their weaknesses and strengths, yet able to withdraw a vision of the world from themselves. When the scientist attempts to identify unity and order, it is not surprising that the pattern he uses is a human pattern ringing with familiarity; it is the same basic structure which has been used countless times in the past by the poets, shamans, and mystics of the world. The result is a curious amalgam of man's instinctive playfulness and nature's endless bounty. Frequently, in spite of man's self-effacing humility it is an amalgam which works surprisingly well and has powers and secrets all of its own. As a result the universe becomes more mysterious, not less.

NOTES

1. Joseph Campbell, *The Hero with a Thousand Faces* (Cleveland: World, 1956), p. 19.

2. Thomas Kuhn, *The Structure of Scientific Revolutions* (Chicago: The University of Chicago Press, 1962).

3. Mark Schorer, "The Necessity of Myth," in *Myth and Mythmaking*, ed. Henry Murray (New York: George Braziller, 1960), p. 354.

4. cited in Mark Schorer, op. cit.

5. Jerome Brunner, "Myth and Identity," in *Myth and Mythmaking*, op. cit., p. 276.

6. Chogyam Trungpa, *Meditation in Action* (London: Stuart and Watkins, 1969), p. 12.

7. William Butler Yeats, "Among School Children," in *The Tower* (New York: Macmillan, 1928), p. 64.

8. T.S. Eliot, "Burnt Norton," in *The Complete Poems and Plays, 1909-1950* (New York: Harcourt, Brace, 1952), p. 117.

9. cited in C.C. Gillispie, "Newton with His Prism and Silent Face," in *Science and Ideas*, ed. A.B. Arons and A.B. Bork (Englewood Cliffs, N.J.: Prentice-Hall, 1964), p. 112.

10. Ibid.

11. Joseph Campbell, *The Masks of God: Primitive Mythology* (New York: The Viking Press, 1959), p. 170.

12. Adolph Jensen, *Das Religiöse Weltbid Einer Fruhen Kultur* (Stuttgart: Schröder Verlag, 1949), pp. 34-38.

Once when I was with Einstein in order to read with him a work that contained many objections against his theory . . . he suddenly interrupted the discussion of the book, reached for a telegram that was lying on the windowsill, and handed it to me with the words, "Here, this will perhaps interest you." It was Eddington's cable with the results of measurement of the eclipse expedition (1919). When I was giving expression to my joy that the results coincided with his calculations, he said quite unmoved, "But I knew that the theory is correct"; and when I asked, what if there had been no confirmation of his prediction, he countered: "Then I would have been sorry for the dear Lord — the theory is correct."

Ilse Rosenthal-Schneider

Quoted in G. Holton, *Thematic Origins of Scientific Thought*, Cambridge: Harvard University Press, 1973.

Chapter Four
The Responsive Universe

The Voices of Nature

Theseus, the slayer of the Minotaur, found his way through the labyrinth by following the unwinding ball of thread. In many European fairy tales a hero or heroine is similarly guided on a journey by the advice of a helpful crone or an old man sitting by the side of a path through the forest. In the language of physics a free particle is led through space-time by following a straight line. In all of these stories there is a remarkably universal intuition that our world contains a structure which can assist and guide the traveler.

A windowless corridor with silent cement walls has rarely appealed to man as an apt metaphor for the circumstances of his journey through space and time. Rather, our surroundings seem invested with a sort of benign aliveness. Forces emerging from the sides of our pathway encourage us to advance when we are doing well and warn us when we are clumsy. These forces appear in various forms: the inertial forces of Newtonian physics; the help from a Bodhisattva, the individual who has stopped just short of nirvana and has returned to aid others in reaching enlightenment; the incarnation of Krishna when the Hindu departs from his dharma; and the warnings of the prophets of the Old Testament when the people of Israel strayed from the ways of God.

Each of these allegories suggests that the universe can be a persuasive and sometimes demanding teacher. Each is an attempt to describe the nudging which people have experienced while trying to follow various pathways. Some paths were found to be more attractive than others because they involved the shortest distance between two points or required the smallest expenditure of energy in moving between these points. Others appeared more harmonious with natural law, allowing the traveler to flow with the changing patterns of the universe. Others seemed to have an almost humane quality, encouraging and supporting spiritual and personal evolution.

It is important to remember that the situation described by physics is not identical to that of these other traditions. In no sense should we regard our discoveries in physics as confirmation of these religious insights, for physics cannot be applied indiscriminately to the realm of human experience. The universe is not so disingenuous as to repeat itself precisely in its various domains. What we are witnessing is a similarity of response to approximately analogous situations. The resemblance of the imagery is not surprising as it is the product of men living on the surface of one planet, exposed to the same forces, and sharing a common environment. Nor does the concurrence of these independent insights necessarily indicate any ultimate truthfulness of the idea. All are human perceptions, suffering from the common numbness of creatures who can feel only an infinitesimal fraction of the total universe.

One particularly fascinating illustration of this awareness of a responsive universe is derived from the report of interviews by the Danish explorer, Knud Rasmussen, with an Eskimo medicine man, Najagneq. Prior to talking to Rasmussen in Nome, Najagneq had been released from jail for having waged war on his own tribe, killing seven or eight members of his community. When brought to trial, none of the witnesses could withstand his stare; they refused to testify against him and charges had to be dropped. He was described as "a solitary man accustomed to hold his own against many and therefore had to have his little tricks."

When he was in Nome, Najagneq witnessed for the first time in his life a white horse pulling a wagon. The white horse so greatly impressed him that when he returned to his village he described how he had acquired ten white horses as helping spirits, and even though the white men in Nome had killed him ten times, he was able to raise himself from the dead each time by sacrificing a horse.

Mixed with such tricks and outrageous nonsense was a vision which Najagneq described with all the authority and eloquence of a prophet. When asked if he really believed in any of the many spirits and powers he called upon, he replied: "Yes, a power that we call Sila, one that cannot be explained in so many words. A strong spirit, the upholder of the universe, of the weather, in fact all life on earth — so mighty that his speech to man comes not through ordinary words, but through storms, snowfall, rain showers, the tempests of the sea, through all the forces that man fears, or through sunshine, calm seas, or small, innocent, playing children who understand nothing. When times are good, Sila has nothing to say to mankind. He has disappeared into his infinite nothingness and remains away as long as people do not abuse life but have respect for their daily food. No one has ever seen Sila. His place of sojourn is so mysterious that he is with us and infinitely far away at the same time."[1] Thusly in a culture far removed from that of the Buddhist, Hindu, Old Testament, or seventeenth-century Newtonian England we find again this intuition of an ordered cosmos which can play an active role in men's lives.

Free Particles and Straight Lines

As viewed by Isaac Newton, the cosmos was structured in space and time according to a plan which existed *independently* of the matter inside of it. It was as if space had a groove incised in it along which moved free particles, and whenever particles "tried" to depart from a straight line, forces appeared which returned them into the straight groove. In Newton's formal description of the behavior of a free particle, the words are different from those from other cultures but the intuition of the guiding ability of space is similar. The free particle does not wander aimlessly; rather, it continues in a straight line at constant speed. Only when it experiences a force will it depart from that straight path. Conversely, when it experiences a force it is being informed by surrounding space that it is no longer moving along the straight line. Newton's law of motion concerning free particles and straight lines has the advantage that it is accessible to mathematical formulation and therefore to test by experience. This quality of testability makes his law different from the story of Najagneq which cannot be subjected to such scrutiny and therefore must remain a highly personal vision.

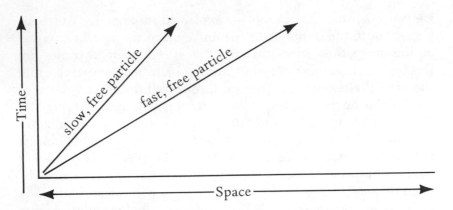

Figure 4-1. The world lines of free particles.

In the world picture constructed by Newton, space consists of a tapestry of straight lines. Free particles move along these lines like beads gliding along frictionless wires. Once a particle is set in motion along its wire of space, it continues without altering speed or direction until it encounters an obstacle. In an infinite universe, the free particle continues to glide effortlessly for eternity.

The paths through space and time of the free particle, the falling apple, the swinging moon, and the earth are called the *world lines* of these objects. People also have world lines, and the whole of one's life can be projected onto two-dimensional space. There on a sheet of paper is a partial representation of our four-dimensional existence. That representation is known as a space-time diagram and is illustrated in Figure 4-1, which shows the straight world lines of free particles. On such a diagram, time moves upward

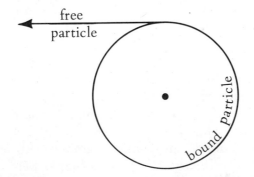

Figure 4-2. The change from bondage to freedom.

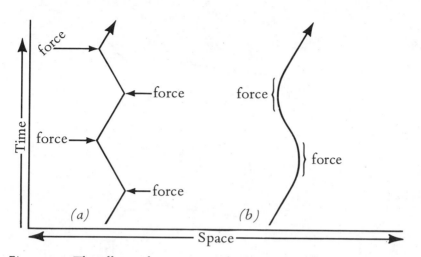

Figure 4-3. The effects of intermittent forces on an otherwise free particle. (a) A series of short-lived pushes produces a zigzag world line. (b) A sequence of longer forces may result in a series of smooth curves.

toward the top of the page and space extends horizontally across the paper. If this coordinate system of space and time is fixed in the earth, then a man leaning against a lamppost is represented by a verticle world line running parallel to the world line of the lamppost. Neither of them are changing position in space but both are nevertheless moving in time. As the man walks away from the lamppost, he is represented by a line which is tilted away from the vertical. The greater his speed, the greater the tilt. When he climbs into a car and drives away, the inclination of his world line increases. The greatest inclination a world line can have is set by the local speed limit and ultimately by the speed limit of the universe — the velocity of light. A horizontal line would thus not represent anything that is possible in our universe, as it would correspond to an infinite velocity.

A ball rolling across the flat surface of a billiard table will follow a straight line unless it is pushed from the side. When so pushed, it curves away from that force. Once the force is removed, the ball immediately returns to a straight line. Newton believed that the curved paths of the moon and earth resulted from the force of gravity pulling on these objects. If that force were suddenly removed, the moon and earth would fly out of the solar system along a straight line (Figure 4-2).

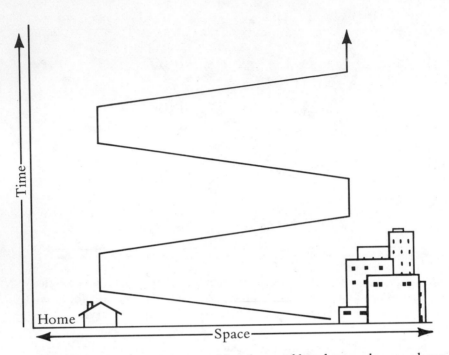

Figure 4-4. With our mixture of freedom and bondage we humans have a variety of potential world lines. One very regular pattern could describe the workdays of a commuter as he travels between home and office.

What is the meaning of this attraction between free particles and straight lines? The answer is remarkably simple: in flat space the straight line establishes the most effective pathway. In going from point A to point B on a sheet of paper, the straight line is the shortest, quickest, and thus most efficient route (Figure 4-5). Other paths are of course possible, but all of them are more expensive in terms of the energy expended and the time required. The free particle manages to choose what is best for it. It is able to recognize straightness and pursues it whenever it can.

In going from a single particle to a system of interacting particles, we find that each system again chooses the style of change which is most efficient. There is a preciseness to our surroundings such that whatever the system, a best route exists. Infinitely many other routes are less desirable, and those are not followed. As the system progresses from event to event, no effort is wasted; it acts in a style such that the smallest amount of effort accomplishes the greatest result.

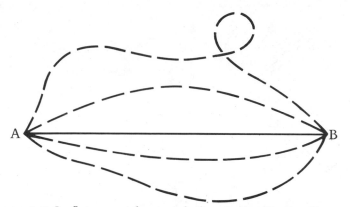

Figure 4-5. In flat space, the straight line is the shortest distance between two points.

The tendency for matter to pursue the most efficient route through space-time is known as the *principle of least action*. In the mathematical form of the principle there is a certain beauty in its conciseness and elegance.

$$\delta \int_{t_1}^{t_2} E(t)\, dt = 0$$

$E(t)$ is the kinetic energy of the system; the integral sign $\int_{t_1}^{t_2}$ means summing the energy over the entire world line of the system from time t_1 to time t_2; the symbol $\delta = 0$ requires choosing that path such that the sum of the energy is a minimum. Here is a remarkably simple description of our experience that systems choose pathways wherein the expended energy is a minimum.

If there is no external force operating on the collection of particles, the principle can be simplified to the form

$$\delta\, (t_2 - t_1) = 0$$

indicating that of all possible paths between two events, the system moves along that particular route for which the time of transit is a minimum. In the field of optics, a similar principle known as Fermat's principle predicts that a ray of light will always follow a path for which the transit time is the least: the principle of least time. In designing a lens for a telescope, for instance, one can locate the focal point by determining the pathways through the glass which require the shortest travel time.

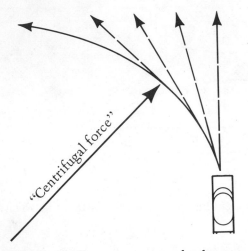

Figure 4-6. The appearance of a force when an automobile departs from a straight line.

The movement of single particles, the development of systems of interacting particles, and the passage of light through space indicate the presence of a structure to space which allows effective action. In its infinity the universe admits innumerable representations of itself, such as this one involving free particles and straight lines, and it continues to encourage man in his role as metaphor-maker. Man has created the metaphor of the web of world lines which he has christened "my universe." The world lines have been extracted from his imagination just as the spider draws from himself the thread that he uses to create the gossamer universe upon which he walks.

An example of the guidance afforded by the structure of space-time is that familiar yet enigmatic centrifugal force which appears when objects depart from their straight lines. If an automobile (Figure 4-6) which is carrying us turns to the left, our tendency is to continue in the original direction. However, we are prevented from continuing in that direction because the side of the car turns and gets in our way. We feel that we are being pushed into the side of the car by a force arising on our left side which is pushing us to the right. The faster the car is traveling when it turns, the stronger the force appears to be.

But while we are sliding across the seat there is no force acting upon us except for that associated with the friction of the seat.

Only when we strike the side of the car and it prevents us from continuing along our straight line do we experience a *real* force. However, when we feel ourselves pressed against the side of the car, we are only feeling the force of the car accelerating toward us. There is no "centrifugal" force pushing us against the car. Were the door of the car to open suddenly, we would fly out along a straight line in the forward direction, continuing to move at a constant speed, not pushed out by any invisible force. When our shoulder is pushed against the door or when we feel ourselves being held in place by our seat belt, we are receiving a message from space informing us that we are no longer moving along the "best" route for us.

Both centrifugal force and its relative the coriolis force, associated with hurricanes and spiraling water in bathtub drains, are known as *inertial forces*. They arise because of the tendency of matter to resist change and acceleration. Likewise, when we smash into the windshield of a car which has suddenly slowed down we experience an inertial force. In each of these situations, we are encountering the ubiquitous teacher residing in the structure of space-time.

The Illusion of Gravity

The universe of Isaac Newton was one of absolute space and time, both of which were figured in the mind of God. The straightness of lines of space was not contingent upon any of the characteristics of our universe but existed apart from the details of the physical universe. Free particles moved along pathways established by a structure which they had no role in determining.

By contrast, in the general theory of relativity space becomes more than a rigid platform upon which the events of the cosmos are performed. Both space and time are active participants in history, with hills and valleys which change with time in response to the flow of energy and matter. Where there is matter and energy, space-time is curved; in their absence, space-time is flat. Gravity as a force has been abandoned, for it is nothing more than a manifestation of the curvature of space-time, and gravity does not exist in flat space-time.

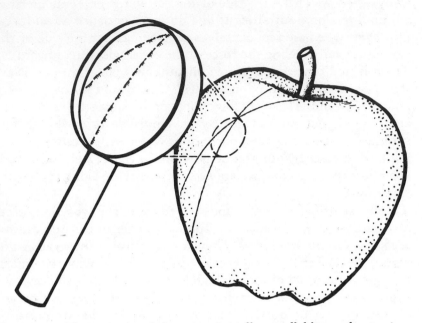

Figure 4-7. The crossing of these two initially parallel lines of ants gives the illusion that there is an attractive force between ants.

Einstein enlarged Newton's concept of the straight-line motion of free particles by inserting the word *geodesic* in place of the words *straight line*. The geodesic is the route involving the shortest distance between two points in four-dimensional space, and lazy free particles choose the geodesic.

As an example of movement along the geodesic, let's return to the fallen apple of the Lincolnshire farm. Several days have passed since Newton saw it fall, and two lines of ants are now moving across its surface. As lazy as free particles, they follow geodesics across its surface. But something happens on the surface of the apple that would never occur on the flat ground. The two lines of ants are at first parallel to each other, and by careful navigation on a flat surface they would always remain parallel, never crossing each other. On the apple, however, with equally careful navigation the two parallel lines will eventually collide (Figure 4-7). To those ants who believe they are still moving on a flat surface, it will appear that there is an attractive force drawing the ant lines together. Actually there is no force at all; on any positively curved

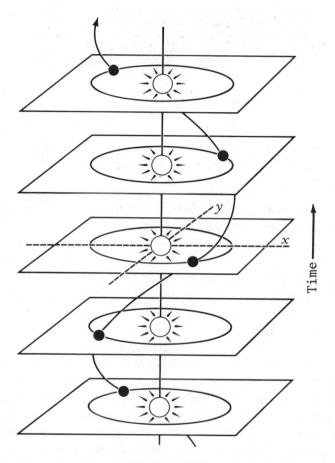

Figure 4-8. The spiraling world line of the earth in orbit around the sun.

surface like an apple, pear, or grape, all parallel lines will eventually cross. But, suggests Einstein, we may be like the deluded ant and mistake the effects of the curvature of space for a "force" of gravity. No force is needed; the only requirement is for space to give instructions to free particles. The moon as it swings around the earth, the earth as it orbits the sun (Figure 4-8), the sun and its companions as they revolve around the center of our galaxy, are all lazily and freely following their geodesics through curved spacetime. The moon is not pulled to the earth by a force, and if spacetime were flat the apparent effects of a force of gravity would vanish.

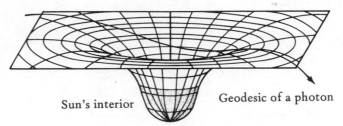

Sun's interior   Geodesic of a photon

Figure 4-9. The path of a photon through the curved space-time in the vicinity of the sun. (After Figure 7-2, "warped space-time" (p. 54) from *Relativity and Cosmology* by William J. Kaufmann, III, Harper and Row, 1973.)

We are part of that curved space, inside it rather than merely living on its surface. We cannot be detached spectators peering in from the outside, for there is no reality outside our universe; if there are wrinkles and curves to space, then we are wrinkled and curved also. We look across the surface of the earth and see our fellow humans walking over its face. And at night we gaze into space and watch stars and planets swinging in vast, curving orbits. They are not cutting through or skipping across the curves of space but are bound to it as we are bound to the earth. As they dip and turn, the planets respond to the hills and valleys of space-time.

The absorption of gravity into the structure of space and the elimination of it as one of the fundamental forces of nature is one of those great and rare syntheses of mankind — a grand, exhilarating metaphor linking two previously independent aspects of the universe. What had been ascribed to an external force is now nothing more than the nimble response of free particles discovering their geodesics in space. The bending of starlight near the sun, which is observed during eclipses, is evidence of the curvature of space-time and not the pull of gravity upon photons of light (Figure 4-9).

We are left with the extraordinary fact that we are not held to the earth by a force of gravity. Our natural tendency is to follow a geodesic in the curved space-time surrounding the earth. In such a state of geodesic motion we would be free like the moon; however, the rigidity of the close-knit crust of the earth prevents us from continuing indefinitely along our geodesic. When we jump from a platform we become momentarily free particles, but we cease to be free once we collide with the earth. The earth thwarts us in our geodesic motion, and it is this state of never-ceasing collision with

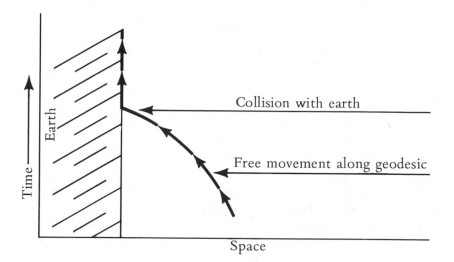

Figure 4-10. The convergence of the world lines of the earth and an apple gives the illusion that there is an attractive force of gravity.

the earth which we experience as the "force" of gravity (Figure 4-10).

Time drives us forward along our geodesic, as blood is driven through our arteries, and it is the earth which is blocking the passage. The physical sensation of gravity is thus a message coming from space informing us that we are no longer moving freely. How strange! Our entire experience on this planet is associated with a clot in the river of time. The crust of that clot, the earth, is sufficiently strong to resist the constant pressure of objects trying to move forward along their geodesics, and they pile up on the earth's surface like flotsam.

Not only did Einstein create an extraordinary unification of nature which burst upon the world of physics in 1915, but he also gave a new and richer meaning to the concept of freedom. Even in the presence of the phenomenon known as gravity a particle can experience freedom, which we now recognize is simply the opportunity to follow the most effective path. In the case of planets circling the sun, their orbits are the manifestation of that freedom; they have chosen the correct path. At every instant of its journey through space-time, a planet or a particle encounters an infinity of alternative world lines. Usually only one is the shortest and most effective, and the free particle and planet wisely choose the geodesic.

Geodesics and Dharma

In the Hindu tradition, the world line — and in a sense even the geodesic — of a person is known as his dharma. Dharma has evolved many meanings: the natural law and order of the universe, the path to perfection, the traditional duties of one's caste, a moral code of conduct appropriate to one's station in life. Dharma has occasionally been singled out as a cause of a degeneration in Indian society, e.g., the encouragement of woodgatherers to remain woodgatherers generation after generation because that is their dharma. Some interpret dharma as a divine injunction against crossing castes. That a concept could be so misused is simply evidence of the power of a human symbol.

There are, however, more optimistic interpretations of dharma, one of which is that dharma is the world line which optimizes personal growth. It is that collection of processes in space-time, infinite in their variety, which encourage evolution in the broadest sense: biological evolution, social evolution, personal evolution. Dharma supports all that is helpful to evolution and discourages all that is opposed to it. It thereby represents all of those processes (not yet described in their entirety by science) which seem to encourage the growth of consciousness in the universe.

In the symbolism of the *Bhagavad-Gita*, the pursuit of one's dharma is an effortless and natural process — just as effortless as the flowing of a free particle along its geodesic or as the cascading of water over a cliff. But unlike the free particle or the cascading water, man possesses a unique gift in that he has the freedom to stray from his most effective path. When people or nations depart from their dharmas, such as when there is suffering, war, or dismemberment of society, forces arise out of nature which tend to restore balance in a manner quite similar to the emergence of Sila. The metaphor in the *Bhagavad-Gita* for those restoring forces is the Lord Krishna who appears on the earth whenever the upward progress of evolution is endangered.

> Whenever dharma is in decay and adharma flourishes,
> then I create myself. To protect the
> righteous and destroy the wicked, to establish dharma
> firmly, I (Krishna) take birth age after age.[2]

There are various ways of keeping people and objects on their geodesics. They are not the ultimate instructions, for like everything else, they are only partial representations born of human flesh; but they appear to be useful. We have just seen that in the expression of the *Bhagavad-Gita* the Lord Krishna appears whenever the natural evolution of the world is obstructed. He became the charioteer of the archer Arjuna and led him into battle as his guide, teacher, and source of energy. Geodesics are means for drawing upon the energy of the universe such as when, by means of its inertial guidance system, the atomic submarine is led through the depths of the ocean by a structure of space-time established by unseen galaxies. It was a geodesic that guided our spaceships from the earth to the moon. But what can we use for our personal guidance system? Since individuals and entire societies can stray, our challenge is to refine our sensitivity to the world so that we can recognize those symptoms of wandering. The ultimate search in the imagery of the Yaqui sorcerer, Don Juan, is for the "path with a heart."

> Look at every path closely and deliberately. Try it as many times as you think necessary. Then ask yourself, and yourself alone, one question . . . does this path have a heart? All paths are the same: they lead nowhere. They are paths going through the bush, or into the bush. In my own life I could say I have traversed long, long paths, but I am not anywhere. . . . Does this path have a heart? If it does, the path is good; if it doesn't it is of no use. Both paths lead nowhere; but one has a heart, the other doesn't. One makes for a joyful journey; as long as you follow it, you are one with it. The other will make you curse your life. One makes you strong; the other weakens you.[3]

Throughout our lives we are capable of choosing between those world lines leading to growth and sanity or those leading to regression and bondage. Both knowledgeably and innocently we make an awesome number of decisions, rejecting an infinity of alternate world lines fanning out ahead of us in time. It is a difficult choice which we are free to make, but it lies at the heart of what a person is. The future course of the whole of creation seems dependent upon our choice since the future grows out of our junctures. Sometimes it seems that more is asked of us than we are capable of providing, and we approach the present with fear and trembling, never quite certain that we are clever enough to learn the guiding language of the world.

NOTES

1. H. Ostermann, *Report of the Fifth Thule Expedition 1921-24*, vol. X, no. 3 (Copenhagen: Nordisk Verlag, 1952), pp. 97-99.

2. Maharishi Mahesh Yogi, *On the Bhagavad-Gita, A New Translation and Commentary* (Baltimore: Penguin, 1969), pp. 262-263.

3. Carlos Casteñada, *The Teachings of Don Juan* (Berkeley: University of California Press, 1969), pp. 105-106.

I do not know what I may appear to the world; but to myself I seem to have been only like a boy playing on the sea-shore, and diverting myself in now and then finding a smoother pebble or a prettier shell than ordinary, whilst the great ocean of truth lay all undiscovered before me.

Isaac Newton

Quoted in B. Hoffman, *Albert Einstein, Creator and Rebel*, New York: The Viking Press, 1972.

Chapter Five

Creative Mythology and
Human Individualism

The Magic of Individuals

The wonder of the universe is that out of the labyrinth of whirling interstellar mists and exploding stars should have emerged man not as a species or as an intricate psychological mechanism, but man as an individual, each man as different from other men as species differ from other species. The miracle is not so much the elegance of these patterns nor even their fragility in a cosmos so violent that it seems to defy the emergence of anything but the huge, hot stars; the miracle is the individuality of man, that possibility of uniqueness which is held tightly between his pulsing temples.

The universe has taken a formless lump of clay and has by now — some ten billion years after creation — demonstrated a few of the infinite variety of forms hidden within that primordial gathering of atoms and forces. That lump of matter has been transmuted with extraordinary skill into the limitlessness that is the human mind. As far as we know, in no other instance within our local universe has inanimate matter been so skillfully worked and has it progressed so extensively by the process of evolution as in the deep spring of human individualism. Ours is an awesome individualism which makes each of us prisoners within our bony skull, forever doomed to be incapable of sharing fully the infinity that is within us.

In his depths the individual is ultimately alone. But he is also ingenious and has devised many techniques for sharing parts of his elusive visions. Each of these techniques — art, music, mathematics, words — operates on different levels and in different individuals may touch different intellectual and emotional centers. Certain symbols shared among groups of people assist the transfer from one to another, and both myth and science are methods for expressing their innermost fantasies.

However, myths are not enough; many people do not find them useful, and others misinterpret their significance. Unfortunately, another technique for dealing with individuality is to deny it. The seduction for self-erasure is strong, coming from within as well as without. More often than not people have found it easier to live under the protection of an established culture in the shadows of old symbols, living the roles and fulfilling the aspirations of others. After all, we are given jobs by other people to do their work, not ours. For a little silver and the promise of security, one may spend the potentially creative hours of his life engaged in the work of others. As the years pass, unless he consciously fights it there is a steady attenuation in his uniqueness. How often does it seem impossible to be an authentic individual and still remain within modern industrial society! How often does the world of organization feed upon and consume the energy of individuals, leaving only discarded shells.

Kimon Friar in the introduction to his translation of *The Odyssey, A Modern Sequel* by Kazantzakis, speaks of man's unmistakable responsibility to take advantage of the gift of his uniqueness: "Each man must consider himself solely responsible for the salvation of the world, because when a man dies, that aspect of the universe which is his own particular vision and the unique play of his mind also crashes in ruins forever."[1]

Despite the apocalyptic visions of those denouncing the current explosion of people, what is needed is not the flawless pill but instead some magical cutters to break the bonds that have been preventing the inner growth of individuals. It is not an explosion of human individuals we fear, but an explosion of interchangeable, mindless sheep, grinning the same faceless face. Judging from the effects of those all-too-rare persons whose minds have swept history — Einstein, Curie, Picasso, Schrödinger, Newton — we need more, not fewer, of such individuals, for it is from them that we have derived whatever grace, purpose, and spiritual strength we now possess.

Those all-too-rare people who have managed to preserve and cultivate their individualism come like magi, bearing gift visions for all mankind. These extraordinary visions rise from an underground reservoir of the human mind. They involve a synthesis of experiences, images, and concepts which no one before had dreamed of relating. It is these surges of creative synthesis which Nietzsche insists must be supported in our fellow men: "That there should ever and again be men among you able to elevate you to your heights: that is the prize for which you strive. For it is only through the occasional coming-to-light of such human beings that your own existence can be justified. . . . And if you are not yourself a great exception, well then, be a small one at least and so you will foster on earth that holy fire from which genius may rise."[2]

These individuals are the pride of the universe. The great spiral galaxies and the brilliant clouds of interstellar gas are no equal for just one of these human beings, for it is from them that we have obtained our eyes to the universe.

The Inner Vision

Einstein has remarked, "The most incomprehensible thing about the universe is its comprehensibility." Its comprehensibility has not been wholly transmitted to us through catalogues of data, the gathering and classification of observations, or detailed photographs of our surroundings. These are necessary but far from sufficient. Comprehensibility has arrived in the form of intuitive hunches, inspired guesses, and flashes of a playful imagination. Contact with the world has generated through the very personal, mysteriously conceived illuminations of a few creative individuals. These illuminations may transpire in a dream as in Kekhule's vision of a snake biting its tail; upon awakening in the morning, as when the problem of absolute simultaneity came to Einstein; or while shaving, as when the technique of holography came to Gabor. It is at these moments that the normal controls of the imagination are weakened and the traditional categories no longer exert their influence. As described by Einstein, the illumination appears in a nonverbal form and develops in the mind like a seed crystal dropped into a supersaturated solution.

The sharing of this inner idea with other people is a secondary step and for many the most difficult. During this stage, an in-

Figure 5-1. The creative moment. ("The Physics Teacher," by Sidney Harris.)

dividual struggling to communicate attempts to carry water from the underground spring of his mind in a very leaky bucket. What reaches the surface is delicious and sweet, but it is a small fraction of what sloshed about originally in that inadequate bucket. Because we are so preoccupied with applying our science and constructing our increasingly intricate technology, we are much like the desert traveler who is given a small sip of water out of a bucket drawn from a well, and who then passes on unaware of the hidden presence of the water remaining in the depths of the well. Those few drops, for all their thirst-assuaging power, are mere hints of what lies beyond words and mathematics.

Locked in every great scientific idea is a mystery. The central image, such as the unity or symmetry of the world, is inexpressible in the precise language of mathematics, and it is all the more mysterious that even a part can be captured in the crude net of science. In *Narcissus and Goldmund*, the artist Goldmund speculates on the presence of mystery in art as he intently watches the water flowing in a river: ". . . one could never make out what precisely was there, but there were always enchantingly beautiful, enticing brief glints of drowned golden treasures in the wet black ground: all true mysteries . . . were just like this mysterious water . . . they had no precise contour or shape: they could only be guessed at, a beautiful distant possibility."[3]

Behind the stern and unambiguous language of great science lies a starting vision, elusive and fragile, glimpsed seemingly only from a distance but felt so strongly that a lifetime may be spent in its pursuit. This initial insight may be on many levels and in many dimensions both in and out of time. Human language is always found wanting: linear one-dimensional language and mathematics, two-dimensional painting, three-dimensional sculpture, multidimensional music. All are underdimensioned compared to that inner mystery; all are partial representations of the inner vision of the artist or scientist. Much is lost in the process of forcing the idea into painted canvas, words, or mathematics, as each is an approximation of that original intuition.

For Albert Einstein the movement from conception to creation was a struggle with mathematics. "Conventional words or other signs have to be sought for laboriously only in a secondary stage. . . . [Then] starts the connection with logical construction in words or other signs which can be communicated to others."[4] Einstein spent the last thirty years of his life attempting, largely unsuccessfully, to express in his unified field theory his grand image of the unity of the universe. Days before his death, visitors found him in his hospital bed still at work with pencil and paper, struggling to give birth to his vision of a unity in physics. He could not communicate it fully because in his estimation he did not know enough mathematics.

Nikos Kazantzakis describes his apparently very similar frustration during his first attempts to write *Zorba, the Greek.*

> I wrote, I crossed out. I could not find suitable words. Sometimes they were dull and soulless, sometimes indecently gaudy, at other times abstract and full of air, lacking a warm body. I knew what I planned to

say when I set out, but the shiftless, unbridled words dragged me elsewhere. . . . In vain I toiled to find a simple idiom. . . . Realizing that the time had not arrived, that the secret metamorphosis inside the seed still had not been completed, I stopped.[5]

The very words used in creative science are from a different language although they may sound familiar. In order to share the vision, new words must be invented or the old ones given new meanings. Words like energy, mass, length, and time — words which seem so fundamental and stable — were given entirely new meanings by Albert Einstein. The new concepts of mass and energy, for instance, did not simply appear, ready to be plucked and gathered. They needed someone to create them so that he could give birth to something inside him. Without him, they could not exist.

> Mass, time, magnetic moment, the unconscious: we have grown up with these symbolic concepts so that we are startled to be told that man had once to create them for himself. He had indeed and he has; for mass is not an intuition in the muscle, and time is not bought ready-made at the watch-maker's.[6]

Joseph Campbell defines this process of extracting images from the individual as "creative mythology," wherein "the individual has had an experience of his own, of order, horror, beauty, or even mere exhilaration which he seeks to communicate through signs; and if his realization has been of a certain depth and import, his communication will have the value and force of living myth."[7]

It is man's peril that whenever he communicates an experience with grace and talent, especially when it is a powerful experience, he is taken too seriously. Because he speaks too well, his listeners forget that before them is merely another creature like themselves: there must instead be some god speaking through this man! How often has the scene been repeated in the flickering light of the campfire circle: the gray-haired elders turn to each other, nod solemnly, and agree, "Yes, he speaks the Truth."

Of course it is not a divine Truth he has stolen from the gods, for he describes only himself and his friction with the moving world. Yet because of their occasional grandeur such human expressions acquire authority and power of their own. As they are retold by others the voice gradually changes its tone from that of an invitation for sharing to a demand for accepting. It is one of the paradoxes of both traditional mythology and of science that these articulate expressions by individuals are used subsequently to control and influence experience rather than to evoke new impressions, thereby discouraging the very process by which the ideas derived their original strength. The effective individuals of this world seem to have recognized human creations for what they are and have thus taken advantage of the license they possess to redesign the old laws.

The Creative Journey

The piercing light of human individualism started a revolution in western science as it flickered in the mind of a canon of Frauenburg Cathedral, Nicholas Copernicus, in the late fifteenth century. The earth had to be set in motion about the sun and the task fell to Copernicus. He could not resist the elegance and simplicity of a planetary system with the sun in the center: ". . . in the midst of all dwells the sun. . . . Sitting on the royal throne, he rules the family of planets which turn around him. . . . We thus find in this arrangement an admirable harmony of the world."[8]

Copernicus was drawn to a sun-centered cosmos by a sense of harmony; thus it was partly an esthetic judgment. Today it seems all too obvious, but in the fifteenth and sixteenth centuries how elating it must have been to discover that the awkwardness of the epicycles of the Greeks could be replaced — that one could actually reorganize the heavens and improve upon the old order! Yet it is striking how difficult Copernicus found it to separate himself entirely from his past. He was divided between the Aristotelian physics of the past and the moving earth of the future. This vacillation experienced by Copernicus was very similar to that of J. Alfred Prufrock, as described by T.S. Eliot. The two men were centuries apart but they shared a classical human dilemma.

> Do I dare
> Disturb the Universe
> In a minute there is time
> For decisions and revisions which a minute will reverse
> . . . .
>
> And would it have been worth it, after all
> Would it have been worthwhile
> . . . .

> If one, settling a pillow or throwing a shawl
> And turning toward the window should say:
>   "That is not it at all,
>   That is not what I meant at all."[9]

It was not the universe which Copernicus was fearful of disturbing, but merely those structures of words which the scholars and theologians used as incomplete representations of our cosmos. But somehow those reluctant wings stirred, and this fifteenth-century Daedalus carried mankind into the uncertainty and freedom of interplanetary space. The earth was launched into orbit around the sun and with it was loosed a cascading revolution which forced man ever more into his individualism. Never again could man have meaning and significance simply because he resided in the unmoving center.

Copernicus caught brief, uncertain glimpses of the motionless sun wrapped by its family of planets, but he could not trust his vision: it may have been a mirage. It is difficult for us so thoroughly accustomed to our peripheral life at the edge of a spiraling galaxy of a hundred billion other stars to understand his hesitancy to urge his vision upon other people. How very difficult it was to trust entirely one's own judgment! In Copernicus' estimation it was safer not to insist, to be cautious, not to wander very far from the old, established ways: "It is fitting for us to follow the methods of the ancients strictly and to hold fast to their observations which have been handed down to us like a testament."[10] When his book was finally published in 1543, the year of his death, it contained a puzzling preface written by Andreas Osiander, the leading theologian of Nuremberg, which advised the reader not to take seriously Copernicus' suggestion that the earth moves around the sun for:

> . . . it is quite clear that the causes of the apparent unequal motions [of the planets] are completely and simply unknown to this art. And if any causes are devised by the imagination, as indeed very many are, they are not put forward to convince anyone that they are true, but merely to provide a correct basis for calculation.[11]

It is not clear how much Copernicus knew of or approved of this preface which was clearly intended to placate the theologians and Aristotelians. However, his years of hesitation so fearful of

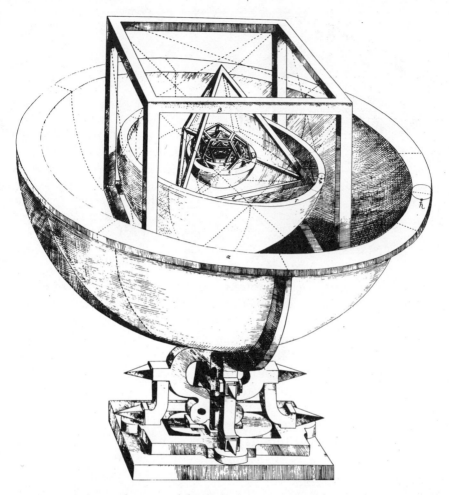

Figure 5-2. Kepler's model of the universe involving the six known planets and the five perfect solids. The outermost sphere is Saturn's, separated from Jupiter by a cube. (From Holton and Roller, *Foundations of Modern Physical Science*, 1958, Addison-Wesley, Reading, Mass.)

ridicule or torment by critics seem consistent with these words of apology for daring to bestir the world. The individual had stepped forward but had faltered and was made pale through thought of consequences. He could not be certain of what he had seen; perhaps there was nothing there at all.

The vision of the "stillness of the sun at the center of the world" did not die with Copernicus; others shared it and one in particular, Johannes Kepler, purified it far beyond the cautious dreams of Copernicus. He was a magnificent, impulsive, always-searching

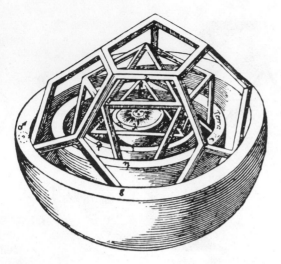

Figure 5-3. The inner planets tightly nestled between the octagon, icosohedron, and the dodecahedron. (Used with permission of Macmillan Publishing Co., Inc. from *The Sleepwalkers* by Arthur Koestler. © Arthur Koestler 1959. Reprinted by permission of A.D. Peters and Company.)

individual: a human being, not a god, who somehow could hear music which had reached few others. He knew he had to embark on a planetary journey but exactly where he knew not, for there were no maps and no one had been there before him.

The starting point for Kepler's journey was at a blackboard in front of his class in the town of Graz, Germany on July 9, 1595. There were six known planets at that time: why only six and what determined their distances from the sun? It must be more than blind, irrational chance that determined the structure of this solar system of ours. On that July day Kepler came upon the idea that the five "perfect" solids of the Greeks with 4, 6, 8, 12, 20 equal sides might be the key to unlock the mystery; they might determine directly the number and spacing of the planets encircling the sun (Figures 5-2, 5-3, and 5-4). Each could be used only once, and hence five solids allowed only six planets. Their distances from the sun as known by him seemed consistent with the respective sizes of the solids. One could not imagine the creator choosing better packing material with which to enclose the planets. In Kepler's ingenious hands there emerged a simple and elegant unity combining planetary orbits, geometry, and mathematics in a unique and unambiguous scheme. The idea was imperfect in most of its details: there are more than six planets; they do not have circular orbits; and their spacings, now known more precisely, are not the same as those of the perfect solids. But for Kepler, aged 24, standing in front of his class and momentarily speechless, it came as a

Figure 5-4. "Stars," modern version of Kepler's metaphor by M.C. Escher. (From the collection of C.V.S. Roosevelt, Washington, D.C.)

"dream of truth . . . inspired by a friendly god . . . [or] heavenly oracle." The vision produced an inner explosion in the young teacher and permanently changed his life.

This event was indeed a case of that individual illumination, the "holy fire from which genius may arise," which according to Nietzsche we ordinary mortals must foster. Kepler wrote, "The delight that I took in my discovery, I shall never be able to describe in words." For twenty-five years he was moved by the impulse of an erroneous idea! It wasn't the idea itself that was at fault; it was his means of expressing it in human symbols. That breath-catching sense of the harmony of the universe which he possessed required more than was readily available from the old symbols. The perfect solids were of Greek invention and nearly 2000 years old; they could not simply be plucked off the shelf and plugged in where needed. They had to be used in more ingenious ways.

As the years passed, assisted by the precise observations of the planets made by Tycho Brahe, Kepler refined and distilled his inner vision. Eventually cast in the medium of mathematics (the first exact laws of nature), the laws of planetary motion emerged from the kiln of his mind. These laws were perhaps the most important part of the foundations upon which Isaac Newton built his theory of gravity, for he used them to test the predictions of the theory.

Through his visions of the planets Kepler had partaken in a psychic interplanetary journey. Almost as in a persistent dream — a dream like that which produced Cooleridge's vision of Xanadu — he moved through the desert of interplanetary space from Mars out to Jupiter and Saturn, out to a region where the sun, which still controls the motion of those planets, has shrunk to a small dot and does little to warm one. In his dream journey described so carefully in his book *Harmonies of the World*, alone among his crystalline solids he experienced the musical harmonies of the planets. Saturn, with a ratio of 4:5 between its maximum and minimum orbital speeds, hummed a major third. Jupiter with a ratio of 5:6 produced a minor third. The space between the planets could not be traversed in person, nor could these harmonies be heard by earthbound man with feet on the shadowed rock of the nighttime earth. But they were audible to Kepler's inner ear.

> The heavenly motions are nothing but a continuous song for several voices (perceived by the intellect, not by the ear); a music which, through discordant tensions, through sincopes and cadenzas, as it were, progresses towards certain pre-designed, quasi six-voiced clausuras, and thereby sets landmarks in the immeasurable flow of time. It is therefore no longer surprising that man, in imitation of his creator, has at last discovered the art of figured song, which was unknown to the ancients.[12]

These are the harmonies described by T.S. Eliot in *The Four Quartets*.

> music heard so deeply
> That it is not heard at all, but you are the music
> While the music lasts. . . .[13]

What made Kepler unique in the ranks of scientists was his extraordinary inclination for introspection and the consequent very careful documentation of each minute stumbling step, each joy, each tragedy of a life constantly beset by poverty and poor health. The sometimes intensely lyrical passages of *Harmonies of the World* have all the appearance of spin-off from a transcendent experience that is inaccessible in its entirety to the world of numbers and words, the full knowledge of which dies with the scientist. Such mystical experiences are not commonly reported by scientists; here we have such a trip initiated by the symbolism of science and mathematics.

In his preface to *Harmonies of the World*, Kepler reflected on his inner, personal journey through mathematics, geometry, music, and mysticism.

> As regards that which I prophesied two and twenty years ago (especially that the five regular solids are found between the celestial spheres) . . . that which sixteen years ago in a published statement I insisted must be investigated, for the sake of which I spent the best part of my life in astronomical speculations, visited Tycho Brahe, and took up residence at Prague . . . finally, I say, I brought it to light and found it to be truer than I had even hoped and I discovered among the celestial movements the full nature of harmony . . . not in that mode wherein I had conceived it in my mind (this is not last in my joy) but in a very different mode which is also very excellent and very perfect . . . But now since broad day three months ago: nothing holds me back. *I am free to give myself up to the sacred madness, I am free to taunt mortals with the frank confession that I am stealing the golden vessels of the Egyptians, in order to build of them a temple for my God, far from the territory of Egypt.* If you pardon me, I shall rejoice; if you are enraged, I shall bear up. The die is cast, and I am writing the book — whether to be read by my contemporaries or by posterity matters not. Let it await its reader for a hundred years, if God Himself has been ready for His comtemplator for six thousand years.[14] (italics added)

For Kepler, numbers — rich and vital — established the pathway along which he traveled. He had sufficient momentum not to be impeded by those bewitching perfect solids or planetary music.

Many persons since Kepler have been imprisoned by these tempt-
resses: the Circes or Calypsos of words and numbers who whisper
sweetly in one's ear that further journey and struggle are not
worth the effort. Kepler was able to drink from their cups and yet
continue his journey.

The Italian Galileo attained a similar degree of individualization
through his personal experience of viewing the planets, the sun,
and the moon through a telescope. He was confident because *he
had seen* with his own eyes, and it was clear to him that the old
authorities were in error. They had not shared his experience. He
had viewed the phases of Venus, which was an impossibility in an
earth-centered universe. He had mapped the pockmarks on the
moon — unthinkable blemishes on such a celestial object. He had
also seen blemishes on the sun; this was even worse. And he had
seen Jupiter with its family of little moons, a miniature sun-
centered solar system available in the sky for everyone to see.
Galileo had seen, had been changed, and became a Copernican.
Unfortunately it was not that simple for everyone, especially for
those whose intellectual growth and flexibility had ceased: some
refused to look through his telescope and others, even after using
the telescope, would not accept or admit what they had seen. The
safe, secure ways of the old myths were preferable to the un-
charted Copernican skies.

Kepler, Copernicus, and Galileo were speaking from intense individual experiences of order and beauty. Thoroughly personal in
origin, the central concepts of modern science — special and
general relativity, quantum mechanics, electromagnetism, the
mechanism of genetic replication — are all, in the words of Einstein, "free creations of the human mind." Based upon ideas not
attained by logical or mechanical processes, these concepts were
the fruits of the intuition and imagination of individuals. These
great revolutionary insights in science were products of minds immersed deeply in the phenomena of nature. Sensitized by a
thorough preparation in the languages of science and fully aware
of the stubborn facts, they were able to take advantage of their individuality.

Certainly many individuals have reached the same stage of
preparation, but few have been able to proceed beyond and create
new science. In this act of creation the individual becomes a re-
cording instrument for the cosmos. Kazantzakis speaks of per-
sonally opening up a riverbed through which the universe may

flow. As Beethoven described the creative act, the spirit spoke to him and he composed a piece. The result of the collaboration is not a cosmic Truth nor mere human nonsense, but rather it is a peculiar combination of the inner fantasies of the mind and the outer phenomena of the world. It is not enough to say that science is more than fiction and less than truth, for it is both and it is neither. Our language is inadequate to describe the science these men created just as our language of quantum mechanics is inadequate to describe the electron. We need to reach beyond language, and that is our attempt in the final chapter of this book.

It is clear, however, that human individuality is essential for the breakthroughs in science. The new connections drawn between the old facts have power which the facts by themselves seem to lack. But mere novelty is not sufficient to attain power. The idiosyncrasy of the individual is needed to make new connections between the old facts. Nor is it enough simply to express that "all is one — the planets and the stars are all related somehow." That idea must be expressed in such a fashion that it can withstand the test of fact. A particular kind of individuality succeeds in science: that which leads to an intuition which works with precision in every known corner of the universe. These are the real breakthroughs in science.

Although today it is less difficult to be an individual than it was for Copernicus or Galileo, most of us live only on the surface of our individuality, never exploring its depth. Our words keep us afloat like giant air-filled balloons. The language we learn in childhood determines not only our style of expression but the very experiences and thoughts which we attempt to express. Our parents and teachers tied our life jackets securely around us, and so we wade in the shallows of our humanness, timid to do more than roll up our pant legs because we feel quite unsure of what lies below. Those few who have been willing to unbuckle their life jackets have returned to become the giants of our race.

Earth-Diver Myths

The experience of individualization has often been described in terms of plunging into that region "wherefrom words turn back" and then rising as though reborn. It is a curiously recurrent motif in many cultures: the Jonah experience of diving into deep waters, perhaps ending up in the belly of some monster, followed by a resurfacing — a sort of rebirth. The Babylonian King Gilgamesh plunged to the bottom of the sea to find and pluck a branch from the plant of immortality. He found it but then lost it after he came ashore. It was subsequently found and eaten by a serpent with the result that whereas man is mortal, the serpent can shed his skin and be reborn. The symbolism of water, fish, and fishermen is strong in the Christian tradition; that of water is close to the idea of rebirth. Baptism may be seen as a symbolic affirmation of the gift of diving that is man's: he has the freedom to escape from the shallows. Christ is symbolized by a fish, and his words to his fishermen apostles continue the imagery: "I shall make you fishers of men," and "unless one is born of water and the Spirit, he cannot enter the Kingdom of God."

Another example of a treasure for which one must dive is the Ring of the Nebelungs lying on the floor of the Rhine. It carried with it, as does all knowledge, a curse of destruction if used for selfish aims. And another ring, the precious ring of Golum, belonged on an island of an underground lake deep in the roots of the Misty Mountains. In Hobbit-like mixture of cleverness and innocence, this ring was discovered by Bilbo Baggins as he stumbled about in the dark caverns near Golum's lake.[15]

These stories of descent into deep waters may be read as allegorical representations of the individualization of man. These are the life-renewing and life-restructuring acts which are exclusively available to the human individual.

The creation myths involving the symbolism of earth-divers are elaborations on this theme of renewal through contact with the energies which lie deep within the individual. The myths involve creatures who dive into the water and reemerge, dripping with primordial slime but bearing remarkable treasures. From the Indians of southern California there is the intriguing story of the turtle struggling to reach the bottom of the ocean.

> Everything was water except a very small piece of ground. On this were the eagle and Coyote. Then the turtle swam to them. They sent it to dive for the earth at the bottom of the water. The turtle barely succeeded in reaching the bottom and touching it with its foot. When it came up again, all the earth seemed washed out. Coyote looked clearly

at its nails. At last he found a grain of earth. Then he and the eagle took this and laid it down. From it they made the earth as large as it is. From the earth they also made six men and six women. . . .[16]

This difficulty of dredging from the depths something new and elusive but a tiny fraction of which exists on the bottom, is an ancient and remarkably common experience of mankind. Formless pre-earth awaits on the floor of that sea which is in everyman, accessible to those who have the courage to make the dive. Out of this dark pre-earth comes light; out of this pre-sound comes the music of people, dogs, and rustling leaves; out of the formless mud emerge those strange human patterns which had no existence before creatures learned the art of becoming individuals.

From Siberia comes the following variation of the same theme.

When these mighty beings descended from heaven they saw a frog (or turtle) diving in the water. Otshirvani's compassion raised it from the depths and placed it on its back on the water. "I shall sit on the stomach of the frog," said Otshirvani, "dive thou to the bottom and bring up what thy hand finds." Chagan-Shukuty dived twice and the second time he succeeded in bringing up some earth. Then Otshirvani told him to sprinkle it on the stomach of the frog (turtle), on which they sat. The frog itself sank out of sight and only the earth remained visible above the surface of the water.[17]

A Rumanian legend echoes the same experience but with an interesting twist.

Before the creation of the earth God and Satan were alone over the waters. When God had decided to make the earth he sent Satan to the bottom of the ocean. Satan was to bring back particles of earth in his (God's) name. Satan dived into the waters three times but did not succeed in bringing back any particles to the surface because he was attempting to take the earth in his own name. Finally, he dived a fourth time in his and in God's name. This time he at least brought some of it up, as much that is, as could remain under his fingernails (or claws). Out of this God finished a sort of cake (a clod) and sat upon it in order to rest himself. . . .[18]

Water in these remarkable stories represents the unformed potentiality out of which the world emerges. It is the creating, fructifying chaos out of which you and I came. Awesome for their

earth-spanning experience, these myths speak of a shared
recognition: man has the ability to dive within himself, to immerse
himself in an ongoing act of re-creation, and thereby has the ability to forestall that life-in-death existence of listless floating in the
secure shallows. In spite of the dangers involved, these creatures
floating on the surface of the sea do dive; they dive alone and many
never succeed in reaching the bottom. When finally one does make
it and returns, most of the earth he gathered has been lost in transit. Much more lies on the bottom than can be dredged up by such
puny and trembling creatures. Much more remains than can ever
be brought up to that flimsy raft floating on the surface of our
waking consciousness where live our friends. That is our fate and
our frustration.

> Turtle was gone a long time. He was gone six years; and when he came
> up, he was covered with green slime, he had been down so long. When
> he reached the top of the water, the only earth he had was a very little
> under his nails; the rest had all washed away. Earth-Initiate took with
> his right hand a stone knife from under his left armpit, and carefully
> scraped the earth out from under the Turtle's nails. He put the earth in
> the palm of his hand, and rolled it about till it was round; it was as large
> as a small pebble. He laid it on the stern of the raft. By and by he went
> to look at it, it had not grown at all. The third time he went to look at it,
> it had grown so that it could be spanned by the arms. The fourth time
> he looked it was as big as the world, the raft was aground, and all
> around were mountains as far as he could see. The raft came ashore at
> Tadoikö, and the place can be seen today.[19]

In this myth, we encounter the loaves and fishes effect whereby
human creations become more than what was put into them: the
tiny ball made of a few grains of mud becomes the earth itself.
Literature, music, and science far surpass in the power of their
synthesis the ingredients taken from the ocean bottom. That ball
of mud grows with a vitality of its own. When we come aground
on it and walk about on its surface, we too quickly forget that it is
all of our own making — that we are witnessing the procreative
power of *our* creations. In these stories, the growing ball of earth
represents the human act of metaphor in which the combination of
physical fact and interconnection swells far beyond the original
components. The measure of greatness of a work of art is the
variety — the entirely unanticipated variety of ways in which it can

move its beholders. Similarly, the great works of scientific art — gravity, Maxwell's equations, relativity, quantum mechanics — far exceed in their applications and influence what their authors could have imagined in their highest flights of fantasy. Newton's theory of gravity, designed for a small solar system, extends the reach of man's mind into the rotating hearts of galaxies and beyond to the horizon of the universe. Maxwell could never have anticipated the application of his equations of electromagnetism from lasers to an understanding of interstellar gas clouds. While we experience the seemingly limitless extension of an idea, we must keep reminding ourselves that we are feeling nothing less than the magical touch of an individual.

The realization of what it means to be an individual is an ancient recognition. It is a deep resonance of man as he discovers he is more than he seems. Not sharing the great survival abilities of the insects, he aspires for more than a secure ecological niche. He does not continue making the same honeycomb in hive after hive, generation after generation. Neither is the web he weaves each sunrise identical to those of all the preceding sunrises. Not all people choose to live their individuality, but when a person does exult in his uniqueness and is able to transfer it into symbols which are meaningful to other people, it is then that life assumes full, rich meaning.

NOTES

1. Kimon Friar, Introduction to *The Odyssey, A Modern Sequel,* by Nikos Kazantzakis (New York: Simon and Schuster, 1958), p. xiii.

2. Nietzsche, quoted in Joseph Campbell, *Creative Mythology* (New York: The Viking Press, 1968), p. 41.

3. Herman Hesse, *Narcissus and Goldmund* (New York: Farrar, Straus and Giroux, 1968), p. 183.

4. Albert Einstein, quoted in Jacques Hadamard, *An Essay on the Psychology of Invention in the Mathematical Field* (Princeton: Princeton University Press, 1945), p. 142.

5. Nikos Kazantzakis, *Report to Greco* (New York: Simon and Schuster, 1965), p. 448.

6. J. Bronowski, *Science and Human Values* (New York: Harper and Row, 1956), p. 46.

7. Joseph Campbell, op. cit., p. 4.

8. Nicolaus Copernicus, *De Revolutionibus Orbium Coelestium* (Johnson reprint 1965, Facsimile ed. of Nuremburg ed., 1543).

9. T.S. Eliot, "The Love Song of J. Alfred Prufrock," in *The Complete Poems and Plays, 1909-1950* (New York: Harcourt, Brace, 1952), pp. 3-7.

10. Nicolaus Copernicus, op. cit.

11. Ibid.

12. Johannes Kepler, *Harmonice Mundi* (Harmonies of the World), ch. 7.

13. T.S. Eliot, op. cit., *The Four Quartets*, p. 136.

14. Johannes Kepler, op. cit., Introduction to Book Five.

15. J.R.R. Tolkien, *The Hobbit* (New York: Ballantine, 1966), pp. 76-95.

16. A.L. Kroeber, *Indian Myths in South Central California*, ed. F.W. Putnam, University of California Publications in American Archaeology and Ethnology, vol. 4, no. 4 (Berkeley: The University Press, 1906-1907), pp. 218-219.

17. Uno Holmberg, *Finno-Ugric and Siberian Mythology*, The Mythology of All Races, vol. IV (Boston: Archaeological Institute of America, 1917), pp. 319-320.

18. Oskar Dahnhardt, *Natursagen*, vol. 1 (Berlin and Leipzig: B.G. Trubner, 1907), pp. 42-43.

19. Roland B. Dixon, "Maidu Myths," part II, *Bulletin of the American Museum of Natural History*, vol. XVII (1902-1907), pp. 39-45.

Nature is a network of happenings that do not unroll like a red carpet into time, but are intertwined between every part of the world; and we are among those parts. In this nexus, we cannot reach certainty because it is not there to be reached; it goes with the wrong model, and the certain answers ironically are the wrong answers. Certainty is a demand that is made by philosophers who contemplate the world from outside; and scientific knowledge is knowledge for action, not comtemplation. There is no God's eye view of nature, in relativity or in any science: only a man's eye view.

J. Bronowski

J. Bronowski, *The Identity of Man*, Garden City, N.Y.: The Natural History Press, 1966.

Chapter Six

The Discovery of Freedom

Scientific Intuition

In previous chapters we described how the universe can be a skillful teacher by establishing pathways for effective action. It tells us when our metaphors are satisfactory by providing tests for our creative fantasies; above all, it yields a never-ending stream of surprises. The universe is all of these and more. To a degree which is sometimes quite humbling, we appear free to design our world, for our reality is an obliging and even docile partner in the hands of a person who understands her.

The most influential ideas of modern physics were generated by a vigorous use of this freedom to design the world. The ideas came from individuals who knew the world but who also possessed a sense of playfulness and a bold willingness to deal freely with the old, established concepts. Such a readiness to innovate was derived from a recognition that in spite of their usefulness and power, our laws of physics are creations of the human imagination. None of the laws are beyond the reach of test by fact. Having been produced by the human fondness for metaphor, whatever validity they possess derives from consistency with past and current human experience. Nothing else gives them accredition.

There are three types of intellectual pleasure in science: the discovery of how a new fact conforms to an accepted model; the discovery of a new fact which contradicts that model; or the most exhilarating of all, the invention of a new model which accommodates the available facts. When many of those uncomfortable facts which contradict a prevailing model become available, science is ripe for one of its rare revolutions. These revolutions are irreversible journeys from one model to a new one, such as when Galileo and Newton broke out of the deductive labyrinth of the

Aristotelians; when Einstein escaped from the deeply entrenched world view of Newton; or when Bohr completely redefined the functions of the archaic Newtonian world machine. In each of these revolutions, the traditional words and images were almost completely renovated. They may have sounded the same and may have had the same letters, but in the new models their meanings were altered. Mass and force, for instance, did not have the same meaning for Einstein as they had had for Newton. Moreover, they were used in ways which would have seemed completely illogical to Newton. Out of the same words and the same terrestrial ingredients emerged a new reality created from the imagination of man.

In our own lives we experience a similar destruction and recasting of our obsolete words and ideas, as in our intellectual development we relive those old revolutions and move concept-by-concept from the flat earth, the rising sun, and the earth-centered universe to the modern view of our less central place in the cosmic scheme. The pain and struggle of education is not so much the learning of new concepts as it is the casting off of the old ones given to us by a variety of teachers. That act of discarding is the essence of the creative act in science; it is the key to the door leading into the next room of our cosmic house.

Freud uses the word *introjection* to label the psychological mechanism whereby parental commands are imprinted upon our personalities. The semanticists point out how the very words of our spoken language determine not only the manner in which we share our thoughts and feelings, but also the patterns of those thoughts and feelings. It would indeed seem likely that the great innovators in physics had somehow escaped significant parental or professional introjection. They were able to confront the world with a beginner's mind, not obligated to accept all of the old symbols or to revere all of the venerable traditions. Consider Albert Einstein's modesty concerning his childlike approach to the matters of space and time.

> The normal adult never bothers his head about space-time problems. Everything there is to be thought about, in his opinion, has already been done in early childhood. I, on the contrary, developed so slowly that I only began to wonder about space and time when I was already grown up. In consequence, I probed deeper into the problem than an ordinary child would have done.[1]

It was a mixture of the freedom of a beginner and the sophistication of the adult which changed the world of physics.

A similar recognition of the need for childlike freedom in the adult world is presented by D.T. Suzuki in his introduction to *Zen in the Art of Archery.*

> Childlikeness has to be restored with long years of training in the art of self-forgetfulness. When this is attained, man thinks, yet he does not think. He thinks like the showers coming down from the sky; he thinks like the waves rolling on the ocean; he thinks like the stars illuminating the nightly heavens; he thinks like the green foliage shooting forth in the relaxing spring breeze. Indeed, he is the showers, the ocean, the stars, the foliage.[2]

What Suzuki describes as childlikeness is also known, I suggest, as scientific intuition: that fecund awareness of how nature operates which results from the mixture of freedom to create new combinations and a total immersion in the details of the world. It is possessed by those who have so mastered their skills and techniques that they have been released from them. The truly creative scientists have somehow managed to escape from being imprinted by the old rules and have avoided that trap of equating successful theory with reality itself.

Zen and Physics

Zen Buddhism is a search for an exit from that labyrinth of words and symbols which has trapped so many of us. Outside its walls lies *tathata,* the "suchness" of the natural nonverbal world. One of the goals of Zen training is the freedom of action which comes from recognition that the world is no longer an inflexible obstacle that must be overcome. One technique is laughter, for it seems that the walls built of our preconceptions can best be broken by humor, and in Zen there is a great deal of poking fun at the world and at oneself. In their use of *koans* such as the well-known one, "What is the sound of one hand clapping?" Zen masters seek to unsettle their students' rigid views and stereotyped approaches to problems. Continually aiming zestful kicks at the seats of pompous students and often playing the fool, the master attempts to engender an openness to the world. No attitude is to be rejected because today it appears silly or unreasonable. For instance, a Zen master said to his disciple, "Go get my rhinoceros-horn fan." The disciple replied, "Sorry, master, it is broken," to which the master responded, "Okay, then get me the rhinoceros." Regarded literally this exchange between master and student is beyond logic, but that is exactly where we must go to find our next model of the world.

In his book *Zen Flesh, Zen Bones*, Paul Reps tells of the Japanese master Nan-in who received a university professor interested in learning about Zen. Alas, the professor was clearly filled with his own notions. While serving tea, Nan-in filled the cup of his visitor but continued pouring tea even as it spilled over the table. The professor watched the overflowing cup until he could no longer restrain himself and called out to stop pouring: "It is overfull. No more will go in!" Nan-in replied: "Like this cup, you are full of your own opinions and speculations. How can I show you Zen unless you first empty your cup?"

The Zen search for freedom in the world is also expressed in the story of the Zen master who was having tea with two students and suddenly tossed one of them a folded fan, asking him, "What's this?" Instead of giving it a name, the student opened it and fanned himself. "Not bad!" was the master's comment. "Now you!" as he passed the fan to the second student, who immediately scratched himself with it, then opened it, placed a piece of cake on it, and offered it to the master.[3] *That* was even better.

A Zen-flavored western story drawn from physics involves the examination question that asks how to measure the height of a building with a barometer. One could measure the atmospheric pressure on the roof and at the ground floor and then estimate the height from the relationship between pressure and height. But a far better method would be to tie a rope to the barometer and lower it from the roof of the building; timing the fall of the barometer tossed over the edge is another good one. The teacher who gives a low mark for such unconventional answers is neither a good Zen student nor a very innovative physicist. The barometer and the fan, as well as our words and concepts, are to be used playfully, ingeniously, and sometimes outrageously. It is only by detaching ourselves from the traditional and stereotyped uses of ideas and objects that physics has advanced.

Experiences need to be accepted without complications. In order to avoid the effects of the excessive classifying and categorizing of the undifferentiated world, we must "know by unknowing." In the command of the Zen master, "Show me the face before you were born," there is a search for simplicity unencumbered by old concepts. The tactics and tricks employed by Zen masters seem very similar to the playful questing and prodding of many good physics teachers, for the solution to many problems in physics resides in being able to discern the situation clearly and simply without preconceptions.

The thirteenth-century Christian mystic Meister Eckhard was in search of a similar openness and freedom from inhibitions: "To be a proper abode for God and fit for God to act in, a man should also be free from all things and actions, both inwardly and outwardly." We are straying from physics, but the point remains the same: the necessary freedom for dealing with the world both physically and spiritually comes from a release from enthrallment by the old symbols. Eckhard spoke of this need for release and how to accomplish it.

> The shell must be cracked apart if what is in it is to come out, for if you want the kernal you must break the shell. And therefore if you want to discover nature's nakedness you must destroy its symbols, and the farther you get in, the nearer you come to its essence. When you come to the One that gathers all things up into itself there you must stay.[4]

Often we do quite the opposite in our classrooms, however, where newer and harder shells are created with the result that the world's "nakedness" is never seen. We learn that barometers are only used for measuring atmospheric pressure and fans are only for fanning. Concepts and theories as they appear in textbooks are frequently groomed to appear absolute and unchallengeable. And the paraphrased words of Isaac Newton, initially evocative and suggestive, have become authoritative, coercive, and inflexible.

In the case of Einstein the oppressive education system under which he suffered for six years in the Luitpold Gymnasium was spectacularly counterproductive. He was outspoken and quite angry about the evils of a Prussian-styled education.

> It is, in fact, nothing short of a miracle that the modern methods of instruction have not yet entirely strangled the holy curiosity of inquiry; for this delicate little plant, aside from stimulation, stands mainly in need of freedom; without this it goes to wreck and ruin without fail. It

Figure 6-1. The innovator in physics like the surrealist recognizes that he is free to deform the old "absolutes" to reveal new realities. Einstein had the courage to distort and reshape space and time although they had become almost sacred objects in the Newtonian world. The above photograph is of "The Persistence of Memory" by Salvador Dali (1931). (Oil on canvas, 9½ x 13". Collection, The Museum of Modern Art, New York. Given anonymously.)

is a very grave mistake to think that the enjoyment of seeing and searching can be promoted by means of coercion and a sense of duty. To the contrary, I believe that it would be possible to rob even a healthy beast of prey of its voraciousness, if it were possible with the aid of a whip to force the beast to devour continuously even when not hungry, especially if the food handed out under such coercion were to be selected accordingly.[5]

The net result of this style of education for Einstein appears to have been a sharpening of his skepticism and his distrust of intellectual authority. Ronald Clark in his biography of Einstein proposes that his reaction to everything the gymnasium represented was crucial in developing the creative man.

If Einstein had not been pushed by the Luitpold Gymnasium into the stance of opposition to authority he was to retain all his life, then he might not have questioned so quickly so many assumptions that most men took for granted, nor have arrived at such an early age at the Special Theory of Relativity.[6]

Skillful Innocence

It is, of course, dangerous to generalize about creative scientists. They exhibit a variety of personalities and temperaments — brash and shy, gentle and aggressive. However, there seems to be a state of mind which one might call skillful innocence that has been prolific in giving birth to much beauty in science. It is that experience of abandonment by a scientist when he plunges into a series of calculations or into an experiment which continues uninterruptedly for days. These are acts of trust when individuals become humble suppliants to the world, never knowing exactly where they will be led during the days and nights lying ahead. The universe has much to teach and one only needs to listen with care and persistence. With nothing to gain or lose (no prestige, no fame, no titles, no dignity) and when there is nothing else but the inexhaustible opportunities of the future, one can get caught up in the flow of the world and can draw upon the energies of that flow. Not surprisingly, good things begin to happen in this state of innocence. Our scientific revolutions have evolved through such individuals who have seated themselves as docile students at the feet of the world.

This experience of *flowing* in the original world before it was structured by man is close to the experience of the religious mystic. When the lights are burning at night in the laboratories of our planet and there is a grappling with a yet unformed world with no search for self-aggrandizement, then the scientist becomes a close colleague with the mystic who has opened himself to his God. Actions performed in such a state seem sanctified; they are naturally filled with good. When St. Augustine comments, "Love God and do as you will," he is speaking of this marvelously productive state of innocence, poverty, and skill.

D.T. Suzuki uses the equation $0 = 00$ to represent the emptiness which is the source of creation: very unmathematical, nicely paradoxical, but how very suggestive! Out of simplicity and poverty emerges the infinite. Possessing nothing more than the cultured skill of a human being, one can indeed do something never before seen in the universe. An even more austere image of the state of creativity is given by St. John of the Cross as he compares man to a window through which the light of God is shining. When that window is clean and transparent and when the glass is of good quality, the undistorted light is seen. Through such a window — through such a person — the energy of the universe can flow. The spattered, fly-speckled window, covered with old theories and prejudgment, impedes the flow.

These are strange words to employ with reference to successful scientists: the light of God, purity, poverty, and innocence! Most active researchers would feel uncomfortable describing their work in these terms. But the important discovery for all of us is that man himself is the most vital ingredient: the human mind is the fertile source of the newness from which science and art spring.

Science like art becomes absurd and impotent when it attempts to duplicate the world; our words and mathematics are inadequate to the task. They can never do justice to nature, always falling short of reality. Indeed, it was not resemblance which was sought in the great scientific revolutions but perfection of the imagery; similarities with the world of physical experience are almost pure "spin-off." Einstein referred with great awe to his experience that a search for inner perfection of his mathematics occasionally would find confirmation in the physical world. For him it was an experience of sacred dimensions that mathematical creations possessing beauty and simplicity should also resemble physical phenomena. That there should be any correspondence between the product of a mathematician seeking simplicity and elegance in his equations and the outer physical world was, for him, beyond comprehension.

The word *innocence* is not inappropriate to use with regard to the experience of pure mathematics. The mathematician is not trying to prove anything. He is immersed in a search for simplicity, balance, symmetry, and purity in the arrangement of his symbols; for him there is frequently reward enough in the beauty of their form. Paul Dirac, a Nobel Laureate in physics in 1933, evinced that beauty was the grail he sought in mathematics. For him it was just that elementary: a search for beauty and simplicity. "It is more important to have beauty in one's equations than to have them fit experiments" (a judgment many experimental physicists would be reluctant to agree with). "It seems that if one is working from the point of view of getting beauty in one's equations, and if one has a really sound insight, one is on a sure line of progress."[7] In the late 1920s Dirac attempted a synthesis of the new ideas of quantum mechanics with those of relativity. His result, the so-called Dirac equation, is a remarkable example of a mathematical idea. It was born innocent of any physical applications yet embodied predictions about the physical world which were soon to be verified. The equation predicted the anti-electron, discovered a few years later; it also demanded a spin for the photon.

The years 1924 to 1927 were extraordinary ones for physics. There was a burst of creativity rarely equalled in the past as men such as Schrödinger, Heisenberg, Dirac, de Broglie, and Born generated the structure of quantum mechanics. The speed and nimbleness with which these men worked and produced enduring ideas is reminiscent of the spontaneity and suppleness of superbly trained artists and musicians. These men, who were creating ideas which were new, bizarre, and so contradictory to the established laws of physics, were met in the late 1920s with guffaws and disbelief from many of their colleagues. They had to be operating out of a state of freedom and emptiness; they could not obtain legitimacy from the old concepts nor much encouragement from many of the older physicists.

We must not be trapped into a binding contract with any of the old laws, no matter how knowledgeable they seem or how great their reputation. They are useful boatmen for only a short distance along the river. Beyond those cliffs in the distance which are approaching only too rapidly, the rocks and pools will be as unfamiliar to them as to us and we shall have to use our freedom to find our own way.

NOTES

1. Albert Einstein, quoted in K. Seelig, *Albert Einstein* (Zurich: Europa Verlag, 1954), p. 71.

2. D.T. Suzuki, Introduction to *Zen in the Art of Archery*, by Eugene Herrigel (New York: Random House, 1953), p. 11.

3. Paul Reps, *Zen Flesh, Zen Bones* (Tokyo: Tuttle, 1957), p. 5.

4. Meister Eckhard, quoted in Thomas Merton, *Zen and the Birds of Appetite* (New York: New Directions, 1968), p. 13.

5. Albert Einstein, *Albert Einstein, Philosopher-Scientist*, Autobiographical Notes, vol. 1, ed. Paul A. Schilpp (New York: Harper and Brothers, 1959), pp. 17-19.

6. Ronald W. Clark, *Albert Einstein, The Life and Times* (New York: World, 1971), p. 13.

7. Paul Dirac, "The Evolution of the Physicist's Picture of Nature," *Scientific American*, May 1963, pp. 45-53.

Struggling slowly, I move among the phenomena which I create, I distinguish between them for my convenience, I unite them with laws and yoke them to my heavy practical needs.

I impose order on disorder and give a face — my face — to chaos.

I do not know whether behind appearances there lives and moves a secret essence superior to me. Nor do I ask; I do not care. I create phenomena in swarms, and paint with a full palette a gigantic and gaudy curtain before the abyss. Do not say, 'Draw the curtain that I may see the painting.' The curtain is the painting.

Nikos Kazantzakis

Nikos Kazantzakis, *The Saviors of God*, New York: Simon and Schuster, 1960.

Chapter Seven

The Magic of Human Creations

Self-Revelation

Our world is constructed of images created and chosen by man. These products of a terrestrial imagination exhibit a strange and seductive power which far exceeds their humble ingredients. Man creates his own reality and often forgets that he himself carved the miracle-generating idols and invented the laws of physics.

The Newtonian theory of gravity has moved a few men to the moon, yet its powers are derived from the synthesis of the human mind and the physical universe. As with all products of time-bound man, Newtonian gravity is incomplete and erroneous. What is ultimately amazing and mysterious about this universe is that in its largeness and incomprehensible generosity, it allows our human theories which are so very wrong to appear so right and permits our ideas which are so pitifully incomplete to wield such extraordinary power.

The failure to recognize our own creations lies at the heart of our current misunderstanding of science. We crouch meekly in front of that power-giving idol, are repelled by it for it seems lifeless and not human, or follow in excited anticipation those mysterious footprints leading where we know not. But somehow, no matter what it seems or whatever disguise it may assume, our science is a self-revelation. As we have been discovering, it is a manifestation of the imaginative powers of mankind joined in a peculiar way with the objects of the physical world.

If Pogo had studied modern cosmology he probably would have remarked, "I have met the universe, and it is us." Actually, the English astrophysicist Sir Arthur Eddington anticipated Pogo's imaginary profundity in 1920.

We have found a strange footprint on the shores of the unknown. We have devised profound theories, one after another to account for its origin. At last, we have succeeded in reconstructing the creature that made the footprint. And lo! It is our own.[1]

A.A. Milne describes a well-known experiment involving the origin of other strange footprints.

"Hallo!" said Piglet, "what are you doing?"

"Hunting," said Pooh.

"Hunting what?"

"Tracking something," said Winnie-the-Pooh very mysteriously.

"Tracking what?" said Piglet, coming closer.

"That's just what I ask myself. I ask myself, what?"

"What do you think you'll answer?"

"I shall have to wait until I catch up with it," said Winnie-the-Pooh. "Now there." He pointed to the ground in front of him. "What do you see there?"

"Tracks," said Piglet. "Pawprints." He gave a little squeak of excitement. "Oh, Pooh! Do you think it's a—a—a Woozle?"

"It may be," said Pooh. "Sometimes it is, and sometimes it isn't. You never can tell with pawmarks."

"Wait a moment," said Winnie-the-Pooh, holding up his paw. He sat down and thought, in the most thoughtful way he could think. Then he fitted his paw into one of the tracks . . . and then he scratched his nose twice, and stood up.

"Yes," said Winnie-the-Pooh. "I see it now. I have been Foolish and Deluded," said he, "and I am a Bear of No Brain at All."

"You're the Best Bear in All the World," said Christopher Robin soothingly."[2]

How perplexing are the equations and related Woozle tracks printed in our research journals. They frequently appear elite and pious as if they came from an alien and nonhuman reality. But they are mere ciphers invented by mankind in an attempt to provide answers to his own questions. The universe is transformed by these questions into a new universe which echoes that question — a universe created by the questioner. In the words of Werner Heisenberg:

. . . for the first time in the course of history, man on earth faces only himself . . . the object of research is no longer nature in itself, but rather nature exposed to man's questioning, and to this extent man here also meets himself.[3]

The Heisenberg uncertainty principle is an example of the manner by which we humans modify by our presence the very world we have created. Electrons swarm about us, enticing us to learn more about them. But when we turn on a beam of light in an attempt to locate these elusive objects, it is much like attempting to measure the temperature of a thimble of water with an ordinary thermometer: the thermometer changes the temperature of the water in the process of measuring. Similarly, photons of light as they shine on the electrons bounce off the particles and alter the velocities of the electrons. As a result we no longer have the electrons with which we started, but instead "new" electrons which have been modified by our curiosity. Whatever we measure, touch, or illuminate we manage to change. The cosmic face that we see amongst the stars and galaxies has been tattooed by human curiosity. Never, according to the standard interpretation of quantum mechanics, can we discover a world which has an existence separate from man. That separate world may exist, but whenever we come into contact with it, it responds and changes.

Even the new, sophisticated electrons built from quantum mechanics are not the ultimate electrons. They are *representations* of electrons — "speaking tubes" that allow us to communicate with that part of the world which we call electrons. The electron in its completeness is still far beyond our powers of visualization. So we assign disguises and attributes to the electron. In one situation it is a particle; in another we see it as a wave. We seem trapped in a Kafkaesque world which seems only to image the curiosity of man. Each time one asks a different question of the electron, one generates a different electron.

In all instances, what we call an electron is an inferior object created by man to represent the superior, as the cross represents Christ but is not Christ. Gravity as a concept is a useful method of dealing with our experience of clinging to the earth, but it is not that experience. So too, the perceptive Greeks recognized that their geocentric cosmos, crystalline spheres, and planetary epicycles were not the real world but only useful conceptual devices. And in Copernicus' book which moved the earth away from the center of the universe, the preface disavows that the theory was ever seriously meant to be more than useful fiction. Although it is not known whether Copernicus agreed with the preface written by Osiander, it is clearly ironical that it was Galileo's insistence that the Copernican cosmology be accepted as absolute fact which caused his trouble with the Catholic church. For at least 10,000 years, the imagination, the gift of fantasy, and the emotional needs of mankind have caused him to try to represent and personify the Absolute. The results have met with varying success, but whether the names be gravity, mass, force, electron, Shiva, Yahweh, or Sila, they were always incomplete representations compared to that which must exist beyond our world and our symbols.

The Expanding Universe

In our attempts in astronomy and in cosmology in particular to describe the universe which lies beyond our local neighborhood, we encounter again this frustrating reciprocity of the world. The familiar universe which is an "expanding system of red-shifted galaxies originating in a big bang" is man-made. It is based upon a number of arbitrary assumptions such as the rigidity of measuring sticks and the uniformity of space. We could not even start our exploration of the universe without having made some assumptions. But different assumptions would result in a different universe, and we cannot be certain we have chosen the correct basic assumptions. In fact, we cannot be certain that a set of correct basic assumptions even exists.

One of the great astronomical surprises of the last fifty years was the discovery of red shifts of distant galaxies. When we peer across our solar system, beyond our galaxy, and finally beyond the fifteen or so galaxies which constitute our local group of gravitationally bound galaxies, we encounter starlight which is always shifted to the red end of the spectrum. All of the galaxies existing outside our local group display the well-known red shift, the amount of which increases with increasing distance. The further we look, deep into space and back into time, we see redder and redder galaxies. At any particular distance we invariably find galaxies with the same red shift; if we look at twice the distance, we see twice the red shift; increasing the distance by a factor of ten increases the red shift by the same factor. This linear relation between red shift and distance, the so-called Hubble relationship, is one of the few cosmic facts we possess (Figure 7-1).

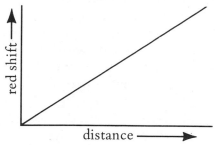

Figure 7-1. The Hubble relationship between red shifts of other clusters of galaxies and their distances.

However, possession does not insure comprehension, and in a perverse way the Hubble relationship tempts us back into a new style of geocentricity. For instance, why are our atomic processes on the earth the bluest in the entire universe? Are we unique after all, surrounded by shells of increasingly ruddy galaxies? We have been burned too often in the past to be tempted into such easy geocentrism. Because of its attractive simplicity, we would much prefer a universe in which all galaxies are equal, all hydrogen atoms radiate light of the same frequency, and all physical constants are uniform.

The Doppler effect has come to our rescue, making it possible for other galaxies to appear redshifted and yet to be intrinsically no different from us. If the red shifts result from the movement of galaxies away from us, then the Hubble relationship indicates that their speeds of recession increase with distance from us. It is thus assumed that the universe is homogeneous and that space expands equally in all directions. As it enlarges like a stretching sheet of rubber, the matter and energy residing in space are pulled away from each other. Every galaxy moves away from every other galaxy, and regardless of the location in the universe, each observer on each galaxy should see red-shifted galaxies in all directions. Astronomers on all of the other galaxies should construct identical Hubble diagrams based upon their observations. Like raisins in an expanding loaf of bread, we see every other raisin moving away from us as the bread is baked. Inhabitants of all the other raisins, except those at the edge of the loaf, should have the same impression.

Other possible models of the universe could have been constructed from our observations, but we have chosen this raisin bread universe because of our desire for uniformity and simplicity. In this model we have also quietly "sneaked in" another assumption, namely that the loaf of bread is expanding and that the raisins are not shrinking. The familiar analogy for the expanding universe as a dot-covered balloon which is being inflated is not an accurate representation of our assumed model. As the balloon increases in size, the distances between the dots on its surface increase, but the size of each dot also increases. Thus, the distance between dots as measured by the size of an individual dot does not change. Similarly, a rubber man living on a dot, with rubber rulers all of which ex-

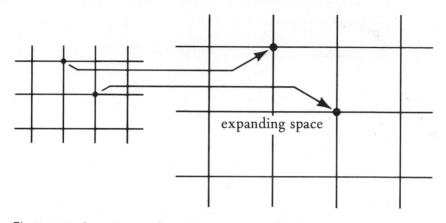

Figure 7-2. Space expands and we remain constant.

pand as the balloon is inflated, would have no awareness of the growth of his ballooning cosmos.

If expansion of our world is used to account for the observed red shifts, then it must be *differential* expansion. We arbitrarily assume that our earth, solar system, galaxy, and cluster of galaxies remain the same size while everything else expands. We justify this difference in the behavior of the small and large by arguing that local forces bind together the small-scale features of the universe, preventing them from being pulled apart by the expansion of space (Figure 7-2).

So far, so good! We have achieved our goal of making ourselves a little island of stability in a universe of change. Yet the fact remains that this interpretation of the red shifts of galaxies is based upon a very terrestrial idea of what is desirable. Were the unit of length to change with time, these red shifts could assume entirely different meanings. In other words, the universe need not be expanding; we simply find it most convenient to assume that lengths are the same elsewhere in space and time as they are on the earth. The Hubble diagram could be equally well produced by a universe in which the large-scale features remain unchanged, but we and our rulers gradually shrink with time (Figure 7-3). Indeed there are an unlimited number of equally acceptable models involving different degrees of expansion and shrinking. All would be consistent with the Hubble diagram as long as the number of ruler lengths separating galaxies increases with the age of the universe.

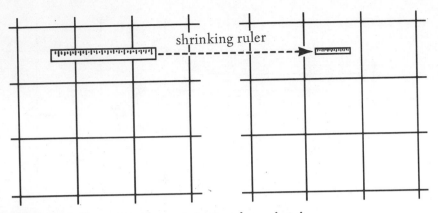

Figure 7-3. Space remains constant and we shrink.

But what a strange and disquieting joke to have played on us! The large and the small of the universe are pulling away from each other, and we are unable to decide whether the large is growing larger or the small is becoming smaller. So by arbitrary definition we have made our rulers stable in length. We like our atoms to be firm and our standards of length trustworthy. Our earth, solar system, and galaxy must neither shrink nor expand. Upon the universe we have imprinted our need to be nonshrinking creatures, and it is that need — that human need — which we see when we look out at our invention, "the expanding universe."

Recently some of the details of this model of the expanding universe have been criticized. Halton Arp of the Hale Observatories has pointed out a number of galaxies which do not conform to the Hubble relationship, i.e., galaxies with large red shifts lying at anomalously close distances. Arp and many other astronomers have also discovered cases of quasars with large red shifts which are apparently close to ordinary galaxies with smaller red shifts. Both observations suggest that not all red shifts can be accounted for by the movement of galaxies away from us in an expanding universe, and that some as yet unknown physical process may be responsible for causing the red shifts. While it is premature to conclude that our standard model of the universe is erroneous, these observations of discordant red shifts suggest that a new model of the universe may soon be needed.

Fred Hoyle and J.V. Narlikar[4] have recently suggested that the mass of particles such as protons and electrons may vary with both time and location in the universe. If, for example, mass decreases with the age of the universe, because of a weaker bonding between electrons and the atomic nucleus the very distant and therefore young atoms would produce redder light than those surrounding us on the earth. Those galaxies which are hundreds of millions of light-years away from us may therefore have large red shifts not because of their speeds but because of the youthfulness of their matter. It is indeed conceivable that the red shifts of all the galaxies in the universe could be produced by this effect of changing mass. Hoyle has also suggested that quasars may consist of particles which have only recently entered our universe, perhaps coming through an Einstein-Rosen bridge from another universe. Such young particles would also have small masses and when contained in atoms would produce red-shifted radiation.

We are, however, not quite ready to plunge into the Hoyle and Narlikar universe. It is not supported by a well-developed theory nor by different kinds of observations. The attractiveness of a scientific idea is not determined as much by its success in describing a single phenomenon nor in making a successful prediction, as by its ability to reconcile diverse phenomena. No alternate theory accomplishes that reconciliation as well as the assumption of a Doppler shift of receding galaxies, for that hypothesis relates to and connects with many experiences on the earth involving matter and radiation. However, although these other cosmic models do not have the persuasiveness of the expanding universe, they remain tantalizing possibilities for future cosmic adventures.

The Curvature of Space

Another case of our dependency upon arbitrary definitions is related to the structure of space. It would seem that a question as fundamental as whether space is flat or curved could be answered in a way which is independent of human definitions. Yet again we need to make an arbitrary assumption about the length of a rigid rod. It is only after we have assumed that all meter sticks throughout the universe have precisely the same length that the structure of space can become a matter of discovery. This remarkable point has been emphasized by Hans Reichenbach in his book *The Philosophy of Space and Time*.[5] If we were willing to tolerate rubbery, curvy, twisty, or telescoping measuring sticks, we could live in whatever cosmic building we desired. If we had a fascination for negatively curved space, we could create a negatively curved universe by making appropriate adjustments to our measuring sticks. But we have decided that a meter stick must be a meter stick wherever it is in the universe, and we have then proceeded with our telescopes to determine what kind of universe is consistent with that assumption. Presently the evidence obtained largely by Alan Sandage with the 200-inch Hale telescope on Mt. Palomar indicates a universe which has a slight positive curvature[6] assuming the rigidity of our measuring sticks.

It should now be evident that our commitment to rigidity is not an absolute necessity. This assumption of inflexibility, which ranks as one of the fundamental assumptions of our western scientific reality, is not to be judged as either correct or incorrect. Based upon the fate of previous similar dogmas such as the "dogma of circles" which ruled Greek cosmology for many centuries, it seems probable that inflexibility will eventually be replaced by a less parochial and more useful doctrine. Now it is an arbitrary decision, chosen for the sake of human convenience and justified on the basis of simplicity.

There is neither any fundamental law which demands that a rigid rod maintain its length as it moves from place to place in the universe, nor is there any way in which we can discover such a change if it occurs. We can detect relative changes between two objects, but it is impossible to prove definitively that a single measuring rod maintains a constant length wherever it may be situated in the universe. Such a rod can always be compared with a second rod at the same place in space. But if that second rod has also changed by the same amount, then, of course, both rods will agree regardless of what has happened to both of them. We return to where we started: absolute length remains as elusive as ever.

The impossibility of detecting absolute changes in length is illustrated in the following fantasy suggested by the French mathematician, Poincaré. Consider a hollow sphere in intergalactic space, in which temperature decreases steadily from the center to the edge. Inside the sphere live creatures which are extraordinarily sensitive to changes in temperature so that they increase or decrease in size with rising or falling temperature, respectively. So sensitive to temperature are they that their size approaches zero as the temperature falls to zero. All other objects within the sphere similarly expand or contract with changing temperature.

Such a sphere would be a closed universe for its inhabitants, a prison with no exit. As they walked to the edge, their bodies would grow smaller and smaller; regardless of how long they walked or how much time they spent in their spaceships, they could never reach the edge. But they would not detect anything strange about their world, for the meter sticks which they carried would also increase or decrease in length in precisely the same manner as did the inhabitants of this strange world. Hence the meter sticks would have all the appearances of being perfectly rigid objects.

If these creatures measured the characteristics of the space of their universe, they would discover that the sum of the angles of a triangle would always total less than 180°, and that the area of a circle would always be greater than πr^2. They would, in fact, conclude that they were living in negatively curved space. An outside observer who could see what was happening in this spherical world would scoff at such folly which led them to assume that their measuring rods were unchanging in length. Yet for them the simplest and most useful assumption to make would be that rigid rods are rigid, and then live with the consequences of negative space. We too must make the same accommodation with our ignorance.

Man-Created Reality

"Reality," remarks Picasso, "lies in how you see things" (Figure 7-4). Our present reality is found in our scientific metaphors, is drawn on stretched canvas, and is built of familiar symbolism. We interpret the world according to the conventions conferred to us by the image-makers of the world. Our perception of the space surrounding us is guided by our symbols. They are not only a means of discovery, intensifying our activities in certain areas, but they are also the enzymes which assist us in metabolizing the world. As our artists and scientists develop and change, providing us with new, more powerful metaphors, we too are remade.

Gertrude Stein once complained to Picasso that his portrait of her did not resemble her. He replied, "Never mind, it will." The American poet Wallace Stevens has explored in several poems this

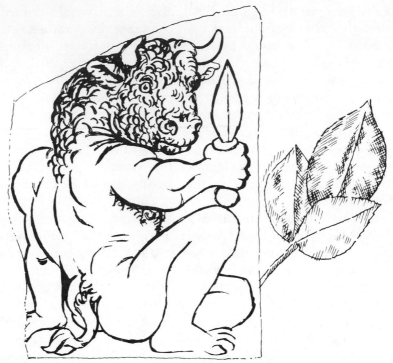

Figure 7-4. A minotaur of Picasso (adapted by Al Burkhardt), possessing many of the characteristics of scientific theory. Standard images are distorted and strikingly conflicting themes are juxtaposed: the leaf, the dagger, and the violent minotaur. A new reality is created by the alien metaphor. (From *The Masks of God: Creative Mythology*, by Joseph Campbell. Copyright © 1968 by Joseph Campbell. Reprinted by permission of The Viking Press, Inc.)

theme of a man-created reality. Reality is so elusive precisely because it is continually being redesigned. How does one decide *how things really are?*

One makes things as they are, Stevens answers.

> They said, "You have a blue guitar
> You do not play things as they are."
> The man replied, "Things as they are
> Are changed upon the blue guitar."[7]

In another of Stevens' poems a girl is singing at the edge of the sea, and in singing she becomes a maker of the world.

For she was the maker of the song she sang.
The ever-hooded, tragic-gestured sea
Was merely a place by which she walked to sing.

The singing girl is sky-maker and ocean-maker. Her song is the world; for her there is no other world. She gives meaning to the sky, the wind, and the waves through her singing. Hers is not a search for absolute truth but an ongoing creation of truth; it is a world created by her for her enjoyment and use.

It was her voice that made
The sky acutest at its vanishing.
She measured to the hour its solitude.
She was the single artificer of the world
In which she sang. And when she sang, the sea,
Whatever self it had, became the self
That was her song, for she was the maker. Then we,
As we beheld her striding there along,
Knew that there never was a world for her
Except the one she sang and, singing, made.[8]

Rarely do we recognize the role we play in creating our world through the manufacture of images and metaphors. But when we cannot identify our creations, we become their prisoners. In an episode of his poem *The Odyssey, A Modern Sequel*, Nikos Kazantzakis explores this theme of the dangers of non-self-recognition. Odysseus, still wandering in this modern continuation of the Homeric epic, was leading his companions southward from Egypt into Africa. At a time when they had been without food for many days, they encountered a native village and devised a strategy to obtain food from the villagers. Out of a partially burned log they hacked a crudely shaped idol and sent their piper, Orpheus, into the village to promise miracles to the natives in exchange for food. Orpheus was instructed to fall to the ground before his rough-hewn god, thrash his hands, foam at the mouth, and most importantly, not burst out laughing. But miracles did start happening and Orpheus, now the priest of a powerful god, soon forgot the origin of the wooden idol.

An old man, blind from birth, screeched "I can see" and wept
A lame man sprang up suddenly on the stones and danced,

....

and as the piper stood in the thick crowd, all pressed
him close, confessed their pain and their pain shrank and died.

Orpheus was undone by the illusion. For him a god was truly
residing in that wooden shape he had so recently helped carve.
Odysseus tried to shake him free.

> "Piper, wake up, an evil dream has poisoned your brain,
> What shame to worship wood! Open your cross-eyes, see
> this is the same domed belley you hacked but yesterday,"
> ....
>
> But Orpheus stared with a dull gaze on his roused master, threw
> himself on the earth and grasped with fear his blockhead god in
> the thick shade of the old oak. [9]

Odysseus was unable to pull Orpheus away from his wooden
god. Men are fragile, he remembered, and too easily lose their
fingernail grip on the slippery world. Saddened by the realization
that he had killed a man by his cleverness, Odysseus moved
further south with his group. Orpheus remained, blinded by his
fantasy, unable to recognize his own crude creation.

Another example of entrapment by our metaphors is found in
that classic situation of childlike fantasy described by Leo
Frobenius.

> A professor is writing at his desk and his four-year-old little daughter
> is running about the room. She has nothing to do and is disturbing
> him. So he gives her three burnt matches, saying "Here! Play!" and sit-
> ting on the rug, she begins to play with the matches, Hänsel, Gretel,
> and the witch. A considerable time elapses, during which the professor
> concentrates upon his task, undisturbed. But then, suddenly the child
> shrieks in terror. The father jumps. "What is it? What has happened?"
> The little girl comes running to him, showing every sign of great fright.
> "Daddy, daddy," she cries, "take the witch away! I can't touch the
> witch any more!" [10]

Usually a child's make-believe is only temporary. However,
many times our pious presentation of physical laws comes
dangerously close to the insistence that the witch and the burnt
match are one and the same when we confuse metaphor with fact.
How often we proclaim by implication: "Our laws of physics are

true and final; the witch is the match; and the match is the witch.'' Some of the current distaste for science comes, I think, from this experience of being shown a match or a wooden god, recognizing it as such, and then being told in all heavy-handed seriousness that we are in the presence of Truth and that there is no room for modifications, alternatives, or contradictions.

It is strange and unfortunate that we seem to be less sophisticated about our scientific inventions than the many "primitive" peoples who can engage in their myths and ceremonies with a mixture of playfulness and seriousness, never fully insisting that the concrete be the ultimate.

> In all the wild imaginings of mythology, a fanciful spirit is playing on the border-line between jest and earnest. (As far as I know, ethnologists and anthropologists concur in the opinion that) the mental attitude in which the great religious feasts of savages are celebrated and witnessed is not one of complete illusion. There is an underlying consciousness of things "not being real."[11]

Much of primitive religion seems to have a strong element of make-believe into which the participants can enter with full awareness of the fakery, not demanding that the festival be either true or false.

> The savage is a good actor who can be quite absorbed in his role, like a child at play; and also, like a child, a good spectator who can be frightened to death by the roaring of something he knows perfectly well to be no "real" lion.[12]

But lurking behind this perfectly obvious recognition that there is no lion, no witch, no god, no gravity, there is the fact that someone has been frightened, that blindness and lameness have been cured by the blockhead god of Orpheus, and that because of our invention of gravity men have been walking on the surface of the moon. In each of these fictions there is an element of truth.

We are surely in touch now with an ancient and stubborn riddle which cannot be easily resolved. Our mythologies, our art, and our science function far more effectively than they should, judging by the smallness of our experience in the world and by the arbitrariness of our basic assumptions. Part of the joy of being a human on the planet earth is the bittersweet realization that in spite of their impressiveness, our creations are doomed to be incomplete and erroneous. It is not the creation by itself which is the pride of mankind, but it is the *act* of creation, for ultimately only the human creative act can never be judged to be wrong. Only the intensity and grace out of which the creation emerged has the chance of never crumbling under the advance of time.

Because it so limits the experiences with which it deals, science can go one step further than art in culturing this riddle. In science, fantasy and intuition are tested by quantitative fact. There is a similar test in art which is made by the audience, but that test is not performed with the same precision as in science. With this style of testing demanded in science, a new dimension of the richness which enfolds us is being revealed.

NOTES

1. Arthur S. Eddington, *Space, Time, and Gravitation* (Cambridge: Cambridge University Press, 1920).

2. A.A. Milne, *Winnie-The-Pooh* (New York: E.P. Dutton, 1926), ch. III.

3. Werner Heisenberg, *Physics and Philosophy: The Revolution in Modern Science* (New York: Harper and Row, 1958), p. 49.

4. F. Hoyle and J.V. Narlikar, *Nature*, vol. 233, 1971, p. 41.

5. Hans Reichenbach, *The Philosophy of Space and Time* (New York: Dover, 1952).

6. Alan Sandage, *The Astrophysical Journal*, vol. 173, 1972, p. 485; vol. 178, 1972, p. 1.

7. Wallace Stevens, "The Man with the Blue Guitar," in *The Palm at the End of the Mind* (New York: Vintage, 1972), pp. 133-150.

8. Wallace Stevens, op. cit., "The Idea of Order at Key West," pp. 97-99.

9. Nikos Kazantzakis, *The Odyssey, A Modern Sequel* (New York: Simon and Schuster, 1958), book XXIII.

10. cited by Joseph Campbell, *The Masks of God: Primitive Mythology* (New York: The Viking Press, 1959), p. 22.

11. cited by Joseph Campbell, op. cit., p. 23.

12. Ibid.

Transience is the backdrop for the play of human progress, for the improvement of man, the growth of his knowledge, the increase of his power, his corruption and his partial redemption. Our civilizations perish; the carved stone, the written word, the heroic act fade into a memory of memory and in the end are gone. The day will come when our race is gone; this house, this earth in which we live will one day be unfit for human habitation, as the sun ages and alters.

Yet no man, be he agnostic or Buddhist or Christian, thinks wholly in these terms. His acts, his thoughts, what he sees of the world around him — the falling of a leaf or a child's joke or the rise of the moon — are part of history; but they are not only part of history; they are a part of becoming and of process but not only that: they partake also of the world outside of time; they partake of the light of eternity.

J. Robert Oppenheimer

J. Robert Oppenheimer, *Science and the Common Understanding*, New York: Simon and Schuster, 1966.

Chapter Eight
The Contrapuntal Universe

The Inseparable Opposites

Although long known by poets, it is a recent discovery of physics that the world seems to be composed of paradoxical combinations. We are surrounded by multiple images which are not reducible to each other and which need to be blended skillfully in the mind with an inner stereoscopic vision. There are, for instance, at least two ways of experiencing time. We all have experienced moments when time has stopped and others when it has raced faster than we ever dreamed it could. Such variability in the flow of time is one of the motifs of Mann's *Magic Mountain* and is treated playfully by C.S. Lewis in *Perelandra*. But in opposition to this experience of supple time, we always hear in the background the monotonous repetition of the ticking of the clock.

Time and timelessness: we cling to a spinning timepiece of a planet and yet are immersed in the timelessness of the ancient photon. Time is an ever-present river which is different each step we make, and it is an ocean accepting the flow of all the rivers of the earth. We are surrounded by transience: our death, the death of our species, the death of our planet, and eventually the fading of our sun. Yet there is a world outside of time in the slamming of a screen door on a summer evening, surf moving across a moonlit beach, or a Grecian urn.

Neither of these two types of experience is sufficient to capture the essence of elusive time. Both are needed. The presence of such mutually exclusive but necessary images is known in physics as *complementarity*. Like Escher's woodcut "Heaven and Hell," life is filled with such pairs of inseparable opposites, neither of which can be neglected without losing part of the world. Such is the Hindu definition of *maya:* the self-delusion that one is in touch with the world when he is embracing only one extreme — looking only at the angel and not the demon. Again and again we must disengage ourselves from the deceptive comfort of enjoying the simple and illusory solution of a dilemma which will never fade.

Death, the last of the many enigmas of our lives, remains even in our modern society a host for conflicting emotions, and many cultures use funerary rites to reaffirm the fundamental dualism of life. Although muted by the efforts of modern mortuary science, the experiences clustered around the act of dying and disposing of the body evoke the strongest set of opposing emotions that we moderns usually experience. Struggling with love for the dead person and the irrational hope that if the body remains he will somehow awaken as if from a sleep, there is the loathing of the formaldehyde-filled corpse and horror of the awful metamorphosis of death. We are torn between opposite methods of dealing with the body, ranging from the permanent destruction of cremation to the mock immortality of lying embalmed in a pink-padded steel vault.

Funeral rites are always charged with extraordinary tension as fascination, dread, reverence, and repugnance joust with each other. The body is a fearful object as it awakens an ancient fear of annihilation. In some primitive societies it must be touched, for in that contact lies a door to the other half of the world. Such can be the final gift of the dead to those left alive. Sometimes the body is stroked, embraced, or kept on the knees of seated persons. In some funeral rituals, the mourners smear their bodies with the fat of the dead person. An extreme example of tension evoked by opposite emotions is found in the rite of sacro-cannibalism[1] performed by the Melanesians of New Guinea. The eating of the flesh of a dead friend or relative is an extreme act of love and reverence, but it evokes such repugnance that it is usually followed by violent vomiting.

Science may also be used as a device for affirming the paradox of human experience. As we have already seen, we encounter in modern physics a similar tension-filled duality: the utter hopelessness of reaching final answers and yet the absolute necessity of proceeding as though they were attainable. Although we have no chance of attaining ultimate truth in science, we must pretend that such truth is available, for how else could we struggle ten to twelve hours a day, seven days a week, year after year in the laboratory or at the telescope? Ultimate success in science is inconceivable. With such a high value placed upon precision and objectivity, ours is certainly the most absurd and paradoxical of human endeavors. As far as we know, nowhere else do people ask such impossible questions or make such unreasonable demands upon the universe. Ours is no modest search, for it is the reconciliation of the entire cosmos which is our goal. We do not ask for that reconciliation which is valid this moment or in this particular and unique situation, but we ask for what is valid always-everywhere. Thus we are wrestling in a ring of primordial hopelessness, with a cosmic injunction against certainty. There is no hope to win the match, but in order to approach our scientific problems with energy and commitment we must continue acting as if we will eventually be successful.

The scientist of today is involved in the same existential dilemma as Harry Haller, the intellectual Steppenwolf of Hesse's novel.[2] Only humor will allow the Steppenwolf to live in a world whose futility he can see only too clearly. Humor is possible, Hesse suggests, only after one has succeeded in confronting at least a few of the conflicts and dualities of his life. Visit the arcade of my magic theater, he encourages, where the rational and the sensual, the logical and the intuitive, the objective and the subjective may be interwoven. A new level of experience in which the polar opposites can be transcended awaits in the arcade where one can abandon the frantic search for Aristotelian certainty.

The fugue is an example of this process of blending opposing themes, and Hesse uses it as a structural form in *Steppenwolf*. In musical counterpoint, two or more contrasting voices are combined, and by their conflict a new entity is created which may be greater than the mere sum of the parts. The intensity of that image and the evocative quality of the experience of listening to the music, increase with the degree of opposition and contrast — to an extreme limit at which they are so different that we are no longer capable of blending the voices.

In such contrapuntal experience, we seek the resolution of the opposing faces of science which we have been exploring, for in that resolution is the promise of an entirely new way of experiencing the world. Beyond the opposing images of science lies the next revolution in man's cognizance of the world. But how is it possible for us, grounded in the logical-objectivism of the modern world, to mix such conflicting images as the logic of modern science and the irrationality of the human soul? Our Aristotelian logic strongly objects to mixing these opposites.

In the wave-particle duality of light discussed in Chapter One, we have an example of this ancient struggle between polar opposites and perhaps also a key to the problem of mixing opposing images. The photon can be used as a contemplative symbol to go beyond the "either-or" way of perceiving the world. The photon is not either a wave or a particle; it is both and it is neither.

The photon is not unique in providing us with such a symbol, for the electron (and, in fact, all particles) needs complementary models to describe it. The electron is also both particle and wave, behaving sometimes like a particle and other times like a nonparticle. In the Millikan oil drop experiment, the electron acts as a single particle carrying a discrete electric charge which is precisely the same for all electrons. The electron seems to be a member of a stream of particles each with a mass of 9×10^{-28} grams when it hits the phosphor of our television tube. Yet when electrons are directed at a crystal, the scattered electrons exhibit a statistical pattern of weak and strong scattering very similar to the light and dark fringes produced by passing light through two parallel slits. The best explanation of these fringes is that the electron has a wavelength like the waves of a violin string or of a swimming pool. That wavelength $\lambda = \frac{h}{mv}$ — the so-called de Broglie wavelength — is possessed by all particles, such as protons, molecules, and neutrons, when they display their wavelike properties. It is only because of the very small wavelength of heavier particles like people or automobiles that we rarely experience their wave nature.

The multiplicity of the universe reveals itself with prodding. The answers we receive from nature depend to a certain extent upon the questions we ask her. The particle-evocative question produces something we call a particle; the wave-evocative question generates that which we call a wave. How very obliging of nature! Yet upon hearing that an electron is both particle and wave, people are unconvinced and mutter: "That is what bothers me about physics. I cannot understand how something can be both wave and particle at the same time. It must be either one or the other. Can't those physicists make up their minds?" And so for some people physics seems to move further away from the everyday experiences of life into an esoteric region penetrated only by an initiated few. But as we have already noted, quite the opposite should happen, for the recognition of the complementarity of electrons returns physics to the human arena where such paradox is already commonplace.

This experience with electrons and photons echoes elsewhere throughout the halls of human endeavor. Complementary modes such as those of death and time can be internally self-consistent and objective in the sense that many people can agree upon them, but they may resist resolution in a simplistic sense. The recommendation from physics is evident: in order to experience it more fully do not force the universe exclusively into one accessible but overly simplistic mold; instead, live with and affirm all qualities.

The Limitations of Language

The reason for the presence of these complementary aspects of our reality resides in the fact that the world transcends our opportunities for experiencing it and far exceeds our ability to represent it with our earth-grown symbols. The nonfamiliar and the non-common-sense must be described by words which were designed for the familiar and the commonsense. Those alien realities must be represented by symbols which carry meanings appropriate only to our human-sized world. The smaller world of the atom must be expanded; the larger world of the cosmos of galaxies must be contracted to fit into our words and concepts. From the distortions arise the paradoxes of complementarity.

Because our style of communication has been devised for man-sized experience, our pictures of electrons and universes bear deeply the distorting imprints of our language. She is a demanding mistress — a preordained pattern into which experience has to be coaxed, cajoled, and finally compressed. Part of the difficulty of our language resides in the intrusive quality of our logic. We penetrate the world of the electron as aliens, blundering about like bulls in a china shop, and we modify the world according to our preconceptions and projections. We assign conventional physical attributes and human logic to the atomic domain.

In his attempts to understand the paradox of the uncertainty principle, Niels Bohr suggested that there is not a unique relation between language and the resulting deformation of phenomena obtained under different conditions. Consequently, word patterns associated with different experiences cannot be combined within a single logical scheme. Independent images emerge from our mutually exclusive experiences. We perform one experiment and obtain one set of results; another independent experiment produces a different set of results. These experiments cannot be combined in a way such that they will mix without paradox.

Complementarity arises, thus, from our inability to generate satisfactory descriptions of the world using a terminology which was devised to describe human experience. We do not even know if we are using the right words when speaking of velocity or position of an electron, and we indeed suspect that we are not. For instance, in the statement that we cannot simultaneously measure the velocity and the position of an electron with unlimited accuracy, it is not certain that an electron even possesses velocity and position, such as does a golf ball rolling across the green.

Do we disturb the velocity and position of an electron when we observe it, or is that just a picturesque way of speaking about a phenomenon that has no similarity whatsoever with a rolling golf ball? The answer offered by Bohr and his colleagues in Copenhagen is that we are probably not justified in ascribing such specific attributes to the electron. All that we have to work with is an inseparable mixture of the object under investigation and the measuring instrument. We should not speak of disturbing the phenomena by observations, for it is doubtful that a particular phenomenon exists without our act of making observations.

Each single experiment is independent and it is incomplete. Bohr argued that the results appear paradoxical because only in the totality of all possible experiments can the mode of being of an electron be described exhaustively. Each individual measurement of the position of the electron is of little meaning unless it is combined with many other measurements. The sum of an infinite series is needed.

What we seek is the electron in its undivided wholeness, and whenever we stop short of that search and try to describe bits and pieces of the electron we encounter paradox. It is not useful, therefore, to speak of an electron which has been altered by the process of measurement, for our only contact with that electron is through phenomena which include both electron and measuring instrument. We have chosen for the sake of convenience to call that joint phenomenon "electron." We never experience The Electron, but only the instrument-electron interaction. In the modern view of quantum mechanics, the electron has no properties when it is not being observed. Its only mode of existence is to be observed. In the process of perception it comes into being for the reason that the object we have named "electron" is composed of various aspects of the process of measurement.

The total electron transcends the language of human physics and mathematics, as does that phenomenon which we call light. The complete electron cannot be described in human words or examined exhaustively by human tools. But our situation is not hopeless: those multiple qualities of wave and particle can be combined in one's mind, as one mixes different vistas of a mountain to attain a feeling for what that mountain is like. At this point — its most sophisticated level — physical theory becomes decisively contrapuntal and almost personal. The beholder is asked to create his own combination of images and to produce something which is as yet inaccessible to the linear sequence of symbols that is our language. For some people the combination can become more than the simple sum of the ingredients and as such it exists only in the mind of man. Never has it been adequately expressed in human language; never has it been written on the pale surface of two-dimensional paper. Indeed no work of art, music, or science has ever succeeded alone, but always waits for the act of human magic to perform the necessary synthesis and reconciliation.

The human ability for synthesis is thus needed to supplement language. The painting is potentially more than canvas and paint just as the electron is more than just wave and particle. In art as in science each statement is incomplete until the nimble mind can mix and reconcile to form a new metaphor which lies beyond language and art. Werner Heisenberg speaks of this strange interior process of blending — a process very reminiscent of the reversing of figure and ground in gestalt with which we experimented in Chapter Three.

> The two pictures are of course mutually exclusive because a certain thing cannot at the same time be a particle (i.e., a substance confined to a very small volume) and a wave (i.e., a field spread out over a large space). But the two complement each other. By playing with both pictures, by going from one picture to the other and back again, we finally get the right impression of the strange kind of reality behind our atomic experiments.[3]

The Intuition of Truth

We are finally at a stage in our discussion where we can embark upon that journey symbolized by a feather for the wings of Daedalus: our journey of creative mythology. As we have seen, our universe is not so simple that it can be described by a single self-consistent model. Since our science attempts to be a mirror for that universe, it does credit to science that it too cannot be captured by a single vision. Neither true nor false, fact nor fantasy, it possesses seemingly undeserved power in making predictions about the physical world. Well wrapped in the paradoxes of complementarity, our physics seems to be at least a step toward that ineluctable reality which enfolds us. The next step carries us beyond the symbols and mathematics of physics — beyond our brightly lit daytime world with its sharp, well-focused edges and logical constructions. Those individual objects which make up much of our world and are so undeniably present are just part of what is available to us. We know them too well; they suit our definitions too precisely. Because we have asked so often "Is it *really* true?" the mythic vitality of our symbols has diminished. We see now only alien, lifeless objects with strange and puzzling powers. Mistakenly we have let ourselves identify these objects with the transcendent power they so inadequately represent.

The true, the real, the sacred is not to be found just beyond physics or beyond art or beyond music. Nor is it fully contained in one single voice of nature singing through mountain pines or across Pacific beaches. It is not just that *or* just this. Nor is it just something one can draw a circle around and say triumphantly, "This is It; I have captured It!" Nor is pure addition enough. The different voices of the universe cannot be tossed into one basket like so many apples, for they would remain single and unconnected. The polar opposites of the world ask much more of us than the simple acknowledgment of their presence.

There is a potentially dangerous trap here. It occurs when one proclaims that the old dichotomies no longer exist and that the resolution of our nagging paradox resides in the fact that all opposites are identical. The polar opposites of the world are not the same, and one should not seek viewpoints which would make them so. No amount of daydreaming, wishful thinking, or doublethink can make opposites authentically no longer opposite, light truly equivalent to dark, or good indistinguishable from bad. They are immiscible like oil and water. Those who proclaim them to be fundamentally equivalent have either not experienced the full oiliness of one and the wetness of the other, or indulgently neglect the details in order to reach an easy solution.

The contrapuntal experience guides us by utilizing the *tension* of the complementary parts. Not only are those conflicting parts to be experienced simultaneously, but the associated tension must be cultured and fully recognized. We must be able to perceive with clarity that the conflicts are undeniable, and we should allow them to trouble us. We should not be allowed to forget that science is contingent upon human history or that science is a myth of our own making. It should hurt that our science of today will eventually be disproven and that our model of the expanding universe rests upon the arbitrary assumption of the rigidity of measuring rods. We should be disturbed that our questions to nature seem to determine the answers we receive and that the complete electron is beyond our powers of visualization. It should deeply puzzle us that the universe as reflected by this kind of science is still abounding in truths: our predictions work; our space probes reach Mars and Venus; the neutrino, black hole, and neutron star do exist.

These opposing images are to be merged as in stereoscopic sight. The fact that one can merge images in a stereopticon does not mean that the original images are identical or that the final image is merely twice as intense as the original images. Identical pictures present no depth perception; the original pictures must be different. The greater the difference, the greater our ability to perceive a new dimension in the pictures.

When one is visually perceiving the world, the dual images which reach the brain are fundamentally different. One image is not derivable from the other; each provides new information which is not available from the other; and each is a mutually exclusive observation of the world, just like our experiences with the electron. The distance between our eyes and our ability for processing the images in our brain usually limit useful pictures to those differing only slightly from each other. But as we know from those times we have experimented with blending stereoscopic pictures, our ability for perceiving the third dimension can be trained and improved. The mystics and visionaries also offer evidence that our ability for blending more complex pictures than simple two-dimensional images can be enhanced.

A technique for developing stereoscopic sight which some societies have found useful involves the use of idols that contain the extremes of the dualistic world. For instance, in the Hindu pantheon of deities the goddess Kali[4] is one of the most ambivalent of all, uniting in her form much that is benign and terrible in our universe. Simultaneously she is the hideous woman who devours her children, and the loving, forgiving, protecting young mother. Wearing a necklace of human heads, she holds above her a bloody sword, and from another hand dangles a blood-dripping human head. Her black tongue is outstretched to lick blood. Yet her two other hands are extended in gestures of protection and forgiveness. After the destruction of the universe, it is Kali who gathers the seed for the next act of creation. Lurking in her uncomfortable form lies the enigmatic power of a cosmos we do not understand, which refuses to let us reduce it to the simple condition of being all good and loving, or all meaningless and absurd; hidden between her terror and ecstasy lie the creation, destruction, procreation, and death of the universe and all creatures.

The statue of Kali may be used as a teaching device, a guide for the searcher, and the fertile ground which the meditative mind can explore. Through contemplation of Kali, who is herself a disturbing, confusing, and obdurate microcosm, the single-imaged facade of the world may be shattered, and for some the mind can momentarily pass beyond the maya of single vision. Next to Kali dances the figure of Shiva[5] who is both the creator and destroyer of the world. In one hand he carries the fire with which he has destroyed countless worlds, and in another hand is his sounding drum which has created all the creatures swarming the earth. Both Kali and Shiva personify, in a variety of forms, the creative and destructive, the vengeful and benign, the ugly and beautiful. Each can act as a device for teaching us contrapuntal vision.

A few who have experienced such vision have returned eager to tell of the wonders lying beyond the separate pieces of the world. Heisenberg used the wave-particle duality of the electron instead of Kali to make the journey. The Buddhist concept of *sunyata* appears to have come from an alien world beyond our everyday

Figure 8-1. Shiva dancing under the halo of flames of the universal con-
flagration. In one hand he holds a drum with which to make the sound of
creation, and in another fire for destroying the world. He dances on the
prostrate body of a dwarf representing ignorance. (Shiva Nataraja, South
India, late Chola period, thirteenth century; bronze, 36⅞″ high. The
Denver Art Museum, Dora Porter Mason Collection.)

experiences: "Form is not different from Emptiness, and Emptiness is not different from Form. Form is Emptiness and Emptiness is Form."[6] The meditative posture of the Zen monk is expressive of an experience beyond labels: "When you sit in the full lotus position, your left foot is on your right thigh, and your right foot is on your left thigh. When we cross our legs like this, even though we have a right leg and a left leg, they have become one. The position expresses the oneness of duality: not two, and not one. . . . We usually think that if something is not one it is more than one; if it is not singular, it is plural. But in actual experience, our life is not only plural but also singular. Each one of us is both dependent and independent."[7]

In the Upanishads one reads, *tat tvam asi*, meaning "This is That." The Christian God who became man, the Word which was made flesh — *Et Verbum car factum est* — requires understanding which passes beyond the things of the world. And those who travel to Nepal hear the chant, *Om mani padme hum*, which means "the Jewel is in the Lotus." Each of these mystifying statements containing complementary images represents an attempt to describe an experience lying beyond words and symbols.

That which is "beyond words" is, of course, ineffable. In his book *The Varieties of Religious Experience*, William James selects ineffability as one of the main characteristics of mysticism. The mystics contend that their experiences cannot be adequately communicated to others who have not had similar experiences. The mystical experience transcends but should not contradict ordinary experience. For the person who is having the experience it leads to seemingly new styles of knowledge, described as a "simple intuition of the truth" or as a "seeing into the sense of things." But when he returns to ordinary life and attempts to describe what happened, most of his listeners cannot understand: "One must have musical ears to know the value of a symphony; one must have been in love oneself to understand a lover's state of mind. Lacking the heart or ear, we cannot interpret the musician or the lover justly and are even likely to consider him weak-minded or absurd. The mystic finds that most of us accord to his experiences an equally incompetent treatment."[8]

Heisenberg's experience of blending the mutually exclusive images of the electron was decidedly mystical. One must know electrons to have the transcendent experience, and the more intimate one's knowledge of electrons is, the more intense the experience. Or in more general terms, if one knows how to use our modern contemplative symbols such as the wave-particle duality of photons and electrons or the paradox of scientific truth, then perhaps one can penetrate that trackless region beyond words as effectively as does the Zen monk or the Christian mystic.

William James refers to transience as another characteristic of the mystical experience. Our trips inevitably end and as in the earth-diver myths discussed in Chapter Three, one must return after a brief dive to his friends floating on the surface. They always ask for a memento of the journey or for some wisdom that might be shared. Many mystics prefer to remain silent; others roar with laughter or speak in riddles. Consequently, it is frequently difficult to determine whether anything significant occurred during the so-called mystical experience. Some observers remain very suspicious of an experience which cannot be fully described.

The scientist, however, needs to be very explicit. He cannot merely say that he experienced the wholeness and the unity of the universe; his insight is not judged to be fully authentic unless he can quantify it in such a fashion that it can be tested. It is not useful to say simply that the planets are all pulled toward the sun by a force, or that starlight is bent in the vicinity of the sun. He must be able to define the force as something which varies as $1/R^2$ and is directly proportional to the product of the masses. Or he must be able to predict that at the edge of the sun, starlight should be bent by precisely 1.75 seconds of arc. Niels Bohr could not be content with only describing the atom as a miniature solar system with a proton in its center and an electron in orbit. He had to use his vision to predict the precise wavelengths of light produced by the hydrogen atom. Then those who have not shared that mystical "intuition of truth" of a Newton, Einstein, or Bohr, can still venture into the physical world and test that intuition.

After a particular scientist has gained credibility by the successes of his intuitions, it is tempting to encourage him to speak in less specific terms about his experiences at the "edge of the world." The world flocked to Einstein after the success of his prediction about the bending of starlight and asked him questions about gods, life after death, the human soul, and countless others in philosophy and theology. Many scientists are not very mystically inclined and are content to let their science remain their primary legacy. A few, including Einstein, have described their experiences, and to them we are indebted for a description of the general features of this inner journey. They speak with a vagueness which is uncharacteristic of their scientific styles, such as when Bertrand Russell, the hardheaded philosopher and mathematician, was drawn to use terms such as the "frightening, wondrous, implacable forces of the non-human"[9] to describe the essential insight of his life of science and philosophy. In a similar vein Louis Pasteur, speaking from his Roman Catholic faith, referred to God as being one form of infinity.[10] Albert Einstein was a rich source of appropriately inscrutable statements, such as his criticism of quantum mechanics as not bringing us "any closer to the secret of the Old One,"[11] and his comment that "We all dance to a mysterious tune, intoned in the distance by an invisible piper."[12] Einstein often spoke of a "cosmic religion"[13] which for him involved a faith in the existence of a fundamental mathematical model possessing great beauty and simplicity which could unify all of the variety of creation.

But, as Einstein cautioned, the result of the journey is to be measured not in how it is described but in how it can be used in the world, for our words are always pale and meager compared with the experience. Judge our mystics, scientific and religious, not by what they say but by what they do. "If you want to find out anything from the theoretical physicists about the methods they use, . . . don't listen to their words, fix your attention on their deeds."[14]

The Esthetic Experience

All of us cannot be mystics, nor do we all aspire to lead scientific revolutions. We are primarily in search of a meaningful and abundant life-style with some beauty and holiness in it. We also need a way of dealing authentically with that physical world which is so rapidly unfolding before our eyes, thanks to the efforts of modern science. In the realm of the theater, each of us has available a training ground for stereoscopic vision needed to cope with the successes and limitations of today's science. The essence of the esthetic experience is the balancing of complementary opposites, and in the theater most of us to a greater or lesser degree have been involved in emotional counterpoint. In those forms of artistic expression where the act itself does not become so fascinating that it loses its transcendent power, one can participate and yet not participate — one can experience terror and yet be free of terror. It is an experience beyond logic and reason: an authentic response to the action on the stage tempered with an awareness of its falsity. As a member of the audience, one does not need to demand that the action on the stage be real — that men actually are pierced with rapiers — in order for the play to be effective. It works in spite of the makeup, the threadbare costumes, and the flimsy backdrops. Of course, the more suggestive the backdrops, the greater the tension between what is being attempted and what is really happening.

However, when the details are too perfectly reproduced and one is fascinated by the experience for its own sake, the paradoxical quality is lost. The experience becomes as simple as that of a child playing with a Barbi doll. The well-formed breasts, "real" hair, stylish clothes, and slender legs of the surrogate world carry no invitation to go beyond, and they steal thereby the opportunity for an adult or a child to cross the line into the world of double vision and counterpoint. The doll by itself is sufficient; it never needs to be more than the molded plastic and painted wood that it is. A matchstick effigy, however, represents something beyond itself.

In the live theater, the experience is more than what is actually happening on the stage. There is no pleasure or excitement or mystery in watching ordinary people walking about on a stage, wearing someone else's clothes, speaking someone else's words, pretending to be somewhere else. The play becomes a uniquely human experience only if the members of the audience can be captured by the fragile illusion on the stage and lose themselves in the drama, thus sharing the feelings of tragedy and joy. Yet one cannot totally lose oneself and abandon all critical awareness; one must, in other words, participate with clarity and precision. There can be no diminution of the pain-joy associated with the dilemma nor an abrogation of rationality, for one must be constantly aware that everything occurring on the stage is pure illusion — all hopelessly false. No matter how much one winces, cries, or laughs, one must recognize that the audience is being fooled and deceived. The greater the clarity with which that illusion is perceived, the greater the quality of the esthetic experience and the closer one comes to entering a new reality.

The person who storms indignantly out of the theater because he cannot understand that "nonsense" on the stage, misses the complementarity of that moment and misses the essence of the esthetic experience. He is not permitting his objects to be anything more than those objects he has defined them to be. No paradox or uncomfortable dilemma is allowed in his world. The man who demands certainty and absolute truth in all with which he is involved, risks not only missing the joy and agony of the theater but also most of life. Similarly in trouble is the naïve child who regards all the action on the stage too literally and plans to ambush the villain outside the stage door. He fails to recognize the illusory nature of the experience.

Consider also the person who is so awed by the power and success of science that he is convinced our laws and hypotheses must be true and absolute. He is able to extract but one meaning from the myth of Prometheus, and he believes that scientists have truly stolen divine fire from the reluctant gods. He equates the masks and the god, the witch and the burnt match, and he finds himself tragically trapped in a rigid and unyielding universe.

These extreme cases fail to attain the balanced movement through the world which characterizes that rare individual who can be enraptured by an idea, direct a good portion of his life by it, and yet not be unduly disturbed when it eventually is shown to be false. Most scientists are accustomed to treat as hypothesis that which others may accept as fact. Yet they are able to operate effectively with a base for action nothing more than an unproven and never to be proved hypothesis. It is possible to become deeply involved in our theories and concepts and use them fully even though they may be largely false. The success of our predictions encourages us to rely upon our physics and to trust it as though it were true. If we were not capable of this little game of "let's pretend," we would be rendered incapable of action, trembling with fear before the inadequacy of our knowledge.

What is necessary in this game of make-believe is the courage to act in spite of the hopelessness of acting. Such is indeed what the existentialists have long been telling us. The creative tension that they seek derives from the ultimate absurdity of a world in which they recognize the need to act as if it were not absurd. Our experiences in physics carry us, I propose, beyond this level of the existentialist dilemma. It is no longer appropriate to label everything as absurd: our physics has been too successful for that.

Standing before our physics we recognize two ancient but enriched opposites: actuality and illusion. It is much too easy to be drawn toward one extreme or the other. But we do not need to choose between these polar opposites. We have learned that absolute certainty and truth are not necessary for effective action in the sciences. We can live with ideas, work with them, and use them to draw energy from the cosmos without being committed to them as absolute truths. Full participation in the world, illumined with the recognition of the tentativeness of its structures, is perhaps our ultimate modern contemplative symbol.

The escape of Daedalus from his island prison was not just a visit to the mainland, nor is our scientific journey simply the exploration of a marvelously luxuriant zoological garden. The significance of both journeys resides in the exploration of the power of a human mind living in this particular universe. Consider everything that our mind has now reached in our physical universe — the wave-particle duality of matter and energy together with our collections of elementary particles, forces of nature, and huge systems of galaxies — and pile these items like pebbles in the sand. They all fit within the island of our human vision, the modest member of an archipelago of realities. Then look beyond at those other complementary realities shimmering and beckoning in the distance. Are they all phantasms, as Kazantzakis suggests, made of "loam and brain";[15] are all those images nought but reflections, and all those sounds echoes? What they *really* are is much less important than how we use them, for that final but unattainable understanding which we all seek is in the words of the Indian Upanishad:

> ...other, indeed, than the known
> And, moreover, above the unknown![16]

NOTES

1. Bronislaw Malinowski, *Magic, Science, and Religion* (New York: Doubleday Anchor, 1954), p. 50.

2. Herman Hesse, *Steppenwolf* (New York: Holt, Rinehart and Winston, 1968), p. 55.

3. Werner Heisenberg, *Physics and Philosophy* (New York: Harper and Row Torchbook, 1962), p. 49.

4. Heinrich Zimmer, *Myths and Symbols in Indian Art and Civilization* (Princeton: Princeton University Press, 1946), and Alan Watts, *The Two Hands of God* (New York: George Braziller, 1963), ch. 2.

5. Heinrich Zimmer, op.cit.

6. Garma C. Chang, *The Buddhist Teaching of Totality* (University Park, Pa.: The Pennsylvania State University Press, 1971), pp. 60-120.

7. D.T. Suzuki, *Zen Mind, Beginner's Mind* (New York: Weatherhill, 1970), p. 21.

8. William James, *The Varieties of Religious Experience* (New York: Random House, 1929), pp. 370-420.

9. Bertrand Russell, quoted in Arthur Koestler, *The Act of Creation* (New York: Dell, 1964), p. 262.

10. Louis Pasteur, quoted in Arthur Koestler, op. cit., pp. 261-262.

11. quoted in Ronald W. Clark, *Einstein, the Life and Times* (New York: World, 1971), p. 340.

12. Albert Einstein, quoted in Ronald W. Clark, op. cit., pp. 346-347.

13. quoted in K. Seelig, *Albert Einstein* (Zurich: Europa Verlag, 1954), p. 44.

14. Albert Einstein, quoted in Philipp Frank, "Einstein, Mach, and Logical Positivism," in *Albert Einstein, Philosopher-Scientist*, ed. Paul A. Schilpp (New York: Harper & Brothers, 1959), p. 286.

15. Nikos Kazantzakis, *The Saviors of God* (New York: Simon and Schuster, 1960), p. 128.

16. *Kena Upanishad*, 1:3.

Index

(Numbers followed by asterisks indicate pages on which illustrations appear.)